Minding Your Family Owned & Managed Business

ENTERPRISE NETWORK
WORLDWIDE

Enterprise Network Worldwide
624 Grassmere Park Drive, Suite 10
Nashville, TN 37211
(615) 377-3392
(615) 377-7092 fax
www.enterprisenetworkworldwide.com

Art by Michael Harris
Cover design by Bozeman Design (www.bozemandesign.com)

Minding Your Family Owned and Managed Business

ISBN 189077717X

10 9 8 7 6 5 4 3 2 1

CONTENTS

Preface

De Boer, Baumann & Company, PLC is pleased to introduce our first book project, *Minding Your Family Owned and Managed Business.* We spent the better part of a year focusing on the family owned and managed business niche we serve in an effort to become a market leader in this area. We analyzed what services had the greatest impact on our clients, and the result is this book and a work plan for small businesses everywhere. We then collaborated with the members of Enterprise Network Worldwide, an accounting association comprised of small- to medium-sized accounting firms, to publish the book.

This book is a compilation of Enterprise Network Worldwide member firms' vast expertise in a wide variety of issues that affect small business owners. Today, the association has over 50 member firms in North America, with a total of over 100 firms worldwide.

The members of the Network are all entrepreneurs, just like you. That's why this book project is important to us. Year after year, we watch our member firms flourish as business owners. They, in turn, help their clients succeed in every aspect of their businesses. Enterprise Network Worldwide members see beyond the numbers to analyze trends, identify opportunities, and strengthen existing business processes for their clients.

Business owners rarely have access to so much timely information affecting the success of their companies or the well being of their families. This publication blends the knowledge and experience of industry leaders from across the US and Canada to offer thought-provoking articles and insightful questions about the issues that matter most to the family business owner.

More than 80% of new businesses fail within the first five years. How do you beat those odds? By spending time working *on* your business, not just *in* your business, and with the assistance of experts in small business management.

The strategies for small business success covered in this book will help any entrepreneur or small business owner think about their business in a new way. Your business has a life of its own. From inception into the future, managing a successful family business requires regular attention and many decisions on your part as owner. This guide was developed to help you pay attention to these areas as your business matures.

We realize that you are busy working *in* your business and that finding time to work *on* your business is not an easy task. This book is organized in small chapters that loosely follow the life of a business. Accountants are most valuable to your company when they are helping you plan for the future. The questions at the end of each chapter are designed to get you thinking in terms of strengthening your business. Once you have thought through the set of questions regarding your company, you should then turn to the "Questions for Your Accountant." By thinking about these questions prior to your next meeting with your accountant, you will be prepared for the session and will be able to get the best return on your investment with your accounting firm.

Browse through the table of contents to determine where you need the most immediate help. More mature companies need to consider different issues than soon-to-be entrepreneurs.

Keep in mind that many small businesses fail to reach their full potential because the owners and managers do not invest the time and resources into building and strengthening the business. Make the commitment to work *on* your business and watch it grow!

We are ready to help you succeed.

Wishing you great success,

De Boer, Baumann & Company, PLC

Minding Your Family Owned & Managed Business

Introduction

Welcome to *Minding Your Family Owned and Managed Business.* This book is based on the contributions of accountants and consultants in the Enterprise Network Worldwide (ENW) alliance. The network is an association of accounting and consulting firms located around the world. By aligning with one another, ENW members can provide better client service across a wider variety of areas to you, the family business owner. For instance, if your company is in Ohio but you also do business in New York, or Canada, or Europe, your local ENW firm can provide one-stop shopping for you.

All Enterprise Network Worldwide firms participate in a unique training program called Five Star Client Service. Among the many benefits of being a member of Enterprise Network Worldwide, this training is perhaps the most distinctive and valuable. By fostering a thorough understanding of customer needs and wants, the Five Star Client Service training program helps Enterprise Network Worldwide members serve you better.

The firms in the network are committed to being your most trusted business advisors. We want to work with you in any way possible to help you and your business. Any accountant can "crunch numbers." ENW firms want to do more for you. By helping you work *on* your business instead of *in* it, we will help you look at your business from a broader perspective and not get caught up in the day-to-day details.

In a way, your accountant can help you have the lifestyle you want. Family businesses are as much about personal decisions and having the kind of life you want as they are about money and "the numbers." We know that running your business is only one aspect of your life. In your business, the issues of growth, succession, and family control are important. But your business is also designed to serve you — to provide the income, lifestyle, retirement, and estate that you want. We want to help you achieve all your goals through your business.

ACCOUNTANTS AS FREELANCERS OR CONSULTANTS

Another way to look at your accountant is as a consultant. You might normally think of your accountant as a source for financial help on topics from financial reports to taxes. That's true enough and in that capacity we act as part-time "employees." We are available to help with a number of topics as you need us. You get high-level help, knowledge about your business, and you don't have to keep us on staff. And because we have experience with hundreds of businesses, we have a broad perspective and can help you with many management issues.

Your accountant may be able to act as a part-time controller, VP of finance, planning consultant, yearly budgeting analyst, cost consultant, and more. When you use an ENW firm as your most trusted business advisor, if we don't have the answer, we have a vast network of experts available to us and will refer you to a proven expert. We are more than number crunchers.

This book is a new tool for us. It is a way to give you some condensed help in one handy package. It is our attempt to open communication with you on a broader, management-oriented basis. Please chat with us about your vision for your business and your wish list of areas you may want help in. We're here for you now and we want to be there for you in even more ways in the future.

OVERVIEW OF THE BOOK

In gathering chapters for this book from members of Enterprise Network Worldwide, we tried to cover a variety of topics that can help you and your key managers learn to work *on* your business, and gain new insight and perspective on your business as it relates to your personal goals. Some of the topics may be useful to you now while others may be relevant later. Many will fit your business, but some will not. We cover topics from what accounting services are to estate planning and personal investments. Most of the topics are issues you might go to your accountant for advice on. However, we also cover topics from marketing to intellectual property.

We believe you will find many of the chapters useful. We've tried to make them brief and to the point. We try to give you enough to help you think about an issue without bogging you down in details. At the end of each chapter we provide questions about the topic to ask yourself and questions to ask your accountant. Our goal is to help you focus your own thinking and to help you communicate better with your accountant and other professional advisors. We believe that if you accept us as your most trusted business advisors, we can use our broad experience with many businesses to help you get more out of yours.

CHAPTER 1

Everyone Knows What Accounting Services Are — Don't They?

The good news is that if you're an entrepreneur who has founded a successful company, you have a gift. Congratulations. The bad news is that your gifts and passion are probably *not* accounting.

What are accounting services? Practically speaking, they are anything your accountant does for you. Depending on the firm, they can range from bookkeeping to computer installations to management consulting. Core accounting services start with bookkeeping as the foundation (although many accountants don't provide basic bookkeeping functions such as accounts payable, check writing, and accounts receivable collections). Often the core bookkeeping is performed within your business and the resulting data are submitted to the accounting firm. This information is then compiled and transformed into financial statements that include a balance sheet, income statement, and statement of cash flow. These financial statements are ultimately used as tools for such needs as business planning, preparation of income tax returns, and so on. Successful businesses have a strong financial foundation with accounting reports and tools that support their long-term success.

FINANCIAL STATEMENTS

Because financial statements are basic to what an accountant does with your business, let's look at a few details of them. Your financial statements are a tool that can help you track every aspect of your business and make decisions about it more quickly and easily.

Despite the fact that most businesses have financial statements prepared and made available to them from either internal sources or external accountants, about 80% of business owners don't understand them fully.

The basic set of financial statements consists of your balance sheet, your income statement, and your statement of cash flow. These can be broken down further over different timelines, product lines, departments, locations, and so forth. In other words, your financials can tell you how profitable a selected time period or product is, and more.

Your balance sheet is a picture of the financial position of your business at one point in time. It presents assets, liabilities, and equity that, when properly stated, can be valuable for long- and short-term planning.

Many business owners look only at the income statement. After all, high profits can make up for — or cover up — a multitude of sins. But all your statements work together as a whole to give you more information. As you likely already know, your income statement shows your financial results for whatever period they are cast for — often a month, quarter, or year.

Most people think that if income shows a profit, they are in good shape. However, your cash flow statement is a crucial piece of the puzzle, and yet is the most overlooked of financial reports. There are different methods of accounting and financial reporting available to business owners. However, no matter what method you utilize, the underlying need for cash flow to fund ongoing business operations never changes. Examples of dangers covered up by your income statement that your cash flow statement can uncover include not having enough income from past sales to finance current sales because of fast growth or slow collection of receivables.

You need to manage your cash flow just as you manage your business. Your cash flow statement will let you reconcile where cash came from and where it went. It will also account for other variables such as non-cash expenses that include depreciation and amortization. Many times the balances in your bank accounts paint a far different picture than the profits or losses reported on your income statement.

LEVELS OF FINANCIAL STATEMENTS

Many small businesses are unsure what "level" of financial statements they are having prepared. And the terms for different levels of statements (compiled, reviewed, or audited) are often misused. When the statements are merely prepared from your internal accounting documentation with no real detailed analysis through application of ratios, inquiry of management, and so forth, they are called *compiled*. Compiled financial statements, as compared to reviewed or audited financial statements, offer no expression of assurance that the financial statements are in conformity with generally accepted accounting procedures (GAAP).

When you are working with banks, investors, or other outside parties, reviewed or audited financial statements are commonly requested. *Reviewed* means your accountants perform analytical procedures and inquiry of management to provide them with a reasonable basis for expressing limited assurance that there are no material modifications that should be made to the statements for them to be in conformity with GAAP.

The highest level of statement is *audited*. Audits check the facts of all items that are material to the accuracy of your financials. An audit consists of your accountant obtaining an understanding of internal controls, testing of accounting records and of responses, observation or confirmation, and certain other procedures (also see Chapter 10 on auditing). Some lenders, bonding companies, and others require this level of assurance. And if you decide to make a public offering of your company's stock, you'll need at least three years of audited statements.

GET MORE FROM YOUR ACCOUNTANT

The resulting product obtained through accounting work is sometimes thought of as a commodity — or as something required of you by others. This is especially true when the financial statements are not adequately utilized in making management decisions, but merely used for tax preparation or a required submission to banks and other third parties. Instead of thinking of an accountant as a provider of a commodity, such as non-utilized, non-appreciated financial statements, there is another way to approach the relationship that can be more useful for you.

Financial statements are only one part of the product and service that an accountant can provide to you. If you could call in top experts only when you needed them for an hour or a day at a time, then you could afford the very best in business consulting such as pension advice, tax advice, succession planning, and more. If you can't afford to hire a high level in-house accountant or consultant, you can benefit from the skills and knowledge of an independent accountant when you need one by having one available via your outside accountant.

In other words, you can outsource certain functions to your accounting firm to free you up for things that only you can do. You outsource functions that you can't justify having internally. Any time it makes more sense to have them in-house, you can bring them in (such as adding a controller — see Chapter 9). This is delegation on a larger scale. There is another benefit to having an ongoing relationship with a trusted outside advisor — perspective. An accountant can help you think "outside the box."

Most accountants want the opportunity to be part of your team. They can bring their experience from analyzing hundreds of businesses to bear on your issues. Scrooge-like stereotypes of old men with green eyeshades bent over ledgers aside, most accountants like to be proactive, and even creative. They enjoy building relationships and helping clients as trusted partners.

BENEFITS OF OUTSIDE EXPERTISE

Let's say that a business consultant came to you and said he or she could help you with marketing, manufacturing, or some other aspect of your business. If you just pay the consultant a fixed sum, for example $10,000, is the consultant sure that you would make or save enough to recover that expense? It would be a worthwhile deal if you were certain that the expense would pay for itself, but you can't be sure. With your accounting firm as a consultant you have an advantage. They already know your business. You've had a chance to build a relationship and learn if their style fits yours. They still bring an outside view and can help you think outside your box. But they know the key performance indicators for your business. They have your financial statements and an understanding of your operations as a foundation to start with.

Sometimes the benefits of the perspective an accountant brings can be very simple but important. Here's an example. Restaurants are some of the toughest businesses to run consistently and profitably. Most mom-and-pop restaurants look at something like their meals from the point of view of a chef, not from the profitability side. An accountant would start with analyzing the financial statements. Your accountant may see that gross profits aren't in line and might then analyze costs and profits from a menu, item by item.

For instance, one restaurant made only a 30% gross profit on entrees but a better profit margin on side dishes. By breaking down the costs on each component of each menu item, we were able to find side dishes that gave the highest profit margin without compromising quality or the chef's goals. By strategically combining the proper side dishes in the proper entree setting, a 60% profit margin was provided which helped overall profitability. More generally in profitability consulting, we look at margins and volume. Some dishes sell more than others do, yet this does not necessarily result in corresponding profits. Volume times profits is a simple equation that tells you your total profits. This is a simple example, but you can see how the average restaurant owner may not think this way.

BUSINESS EXAMPLES

Most entrepreneurs start businesses based on their own passions. But one founder we worked with approached starting a business from a very analytical viewpoint. He had a full-time job as an executive in a trucking company. He wanted to start a business and conducted research on various possibilities. He did his homework and looked at different industries and franchises. Because of his past experience, he saw the value of a business plan and a strong business infrastructure. His planning dealt with human resources, accounting, financing, capital requirements, and many details that are often overlooked by entrepreneurs. He worked with his bank and accountant to run projections and set conservative goals. He knew what cash flow was needed to repay debt. He also considered future expansion. He maintained his trucking company job for a few years while his son ran the business. During this time he closely compared and monitored actual business operating results against his original business plan and projections. He had strong financial reporting practices in place and planned in a manner that laid the foundations for marketing, internal controls, and human resources that would have worked in any business setting.

The business venture in the above example was dry cleaning, but it doesn't matter what type of industry this was — what matters is the effort and forethought that went into planning the operations. He started with one location and soon had multiple locations. He achieved, and has maintained, entrepreneurial success. The strong commitment to detailed planning provided the framework for his success. This success allowed him the opportunity and ability to quit his job as an executive in the trucking company and enter full time in the family business. Thus, he achieved every working person's dream!

On the other hand, a different business made a number of simple mistakes that cost them dearly. We were compiling quarterly financial statements for them and processing payroll, but they didn't want to spend the money for monthly financials and further in-depth consulting services. The quarterly statements were always behind due to the client's lack of effort in supplying timely information and therefore we were always evaluating old, outdated results of the company's financial performance. For years they survived, but profits were up and down with a flat trend. Eventually they had a period where volume was up, but not profits.

When we were finally given the opportunity to analyze their

situation, the source of their underlying problem was apparent: They didn't understand gross profit margin versus markup percentage. Retailers often use a certain percentage markup called *keystone:* taking the wholesale price of the item and doubling it to determine the retail price (for example, a $1 item would retail for $2).

This particular business understood they needed a 50% *gross profit percentage* to be profitable or at least break even. They thought that a 50% markup would result in a 50% gross profit and therefore had been taking a $1 item and marking it up to $1.50. They thought this would produce a gross profit result of 50% of their selling price. The actual result of a 50% markup is a gross profit of 33% (gross profit percentage is calculated from the retail price of the item, so this business was making only 50¢ on a $1.50 sale, or 33%).

As you can plainly see, their methodology was only producing 33% gross profit (50¢), while all along they thought it was producing 50% (75¢). Only a 100% markup (keystone) would result in a 50% gross profit (that is, with a $1 item marked up 100% to $2, you make $1 on a $2 sale — 50%). With a faulty understanding of their financials, it was no wonder there were not corresponding net company profits coming from their increase in overall sales volume.

After helping them understand this problem, they raised prices to a 100% markup in order to meet their goal of 50% gross profit (they didn't lose gross sales volume because they were still at or below market pricing) and generated higher net company profits than they had ever previously generated. This situation is an instance where understanding or misunderstanding the meaning and application of a single simple financial accounting concept was the deciding factor in the survival of this enterprise.

The three simplest keys to analyzing your financial success are:

- Volume to projections
- Your cost of goods and gross margins
- Your selling, general, and administrative expenses (overhead: SG&A)

By the way, many times it takes a problem to get you to focus attention on what is going wrong so you can fix it. That's a natural tendency. However, as a general tip, it's worth analyzing the things that you're doing well. Often they make up the biggest part of your business so changes have the most impact there. And often it's much more profitable to improve something that's going well than to fix something that's going badly. Problems can attract too much time and you need to leverage your time for the most profits.

CONCLUSION

Accounting services seem dull, expensive, or intimidating to many business owners. It's easy for entrepreneurs to focus on the bread-and-butter aspects of running their businesses and let their financial statements and accounting get behind. But this means they don't have up-to-date information as a reporting or planning tool. That's too bad because "the numbers" can be your best business tool.

Instead of thinking of financial statements as things that you *have* to have, think of them as tools that can help you run your business better. Of course, accountants *do* work on your financials; however, most good accountants are interested in helping you with your overall business. Try thinking of them as part-time experts on your business who are available just when you need them. You (and they) may enjoy the fuller business relationship.

QUESTIONS TO ASK YOURSELF

1. Do I understand the importance of financial reporting and accounting functions in my business? Do I see the value equal to other aspects of the business such as the areas of selling, production, and so on?

2. Can I read and understand my financial statements?

3. Are they useful to me for management decisions?

4. What are my key performance indicators (KPIs) — the shortcuts to monitor where I am financially?

5. Am I recording and relying on these KPIs?

6. Do I have an easy way to regularly measure and monitor my cash flow as compared to profitability?

7. Can I do a breakeven analysis to measure survival?

8. Am I comfortable with my accountant on a personal basis?

9. Is my accountant proactive in suggesting how to improve my business?

10. Have I surrounded myself with a team of professionals for which I am confident in and trust?

11. Do I have a sound business plan and strategic plan that incorporate strong financial objectives?

QUESTIONS TO ASK YOUR ACCOUNTANT

1. What key ratios or KPIs can you show me to watch in my business?

2. Are you familiar with my industry?

3. How do you stay on top of new developments in my industry?

4. Do you feel comfortable with me?

5. Can you support our company culture and values?

6. Can I meet your team that I'll be working with? [You're looking for a long-term perspective here.]

7. Will you make yourself available for me when I need advice?

8. Are you a number cruncher or a number communicator? I need someone who can communicate and consult with me on anything from simple to complex business matters.

CHAPTER 2

Who Needs Accounting Systems?

When you started your business, you probably performed all of the activities of the business and were intimately familiar with what was happening. However, after a time you can't keep everything in your head. One of the most important things to document properly is your money. That's essentially what your accounting system does.

Timely information about key operating statistics is critical to the long-term success of your business. Your accounting system is designed to serve you first, and then to report to others. As soon as you hire your first employee, you no longer have first-hand information about everything that occurs in the business, and neither does that employee. Your accounting system is also a management information system that makes the information you and others need available.

People outside of your business who you interact with, such as customers and vendors, and the entities that you must report to, such as the tax collection agencies, state or provincial agencies, banks, and insurance companies, also require information about your business. Your financial statements are key in your dealings with these entities.

The goals of your accounting system go beyond reporting information to various parties. How many times have you read articles about trusted employees who were stealing money from the businesses they worked for over a period of years? An important part of an accounting system is to protect your company's assets. According to the Association of Certified Fraud Examiners in its 2004 *Report to the Nation on Occupational Fraud and Abuse,* the average organization loses about six percent of its total annual revenue to fraud and abuse committed by its own employees. The Association also found that the median cost for small businesses was higher than for all but the very largest businesses.

Finally, if you decide to sell your business, reliable, accurate financial statements and other accounting information will be one of your best tools to get top dollar.

WHAT SHOULD MY COMPANY'S FINANCIAL STATEMENTS INCLUDE?

The SEC, the AICPA, and generally accepted accounting standards state that you — not your accountant or auditor — are responsible for your company's financial statements and the representations included in them. Those representations include the following:

Existence and occurrence: The recorded transactions existed or occurred at a given date or within a given period.

Completeness: All the transactions that occurred or existed and should have been recorded are in fact recorded.

Rights and obligations: All assets to which the company has a right are recorded and none other. All liabilities to which the company is obligated are recorded.

Valuation and allocation: All the transactions are recorded at appropriate amounts.

Presentation and disclosure: All components of the financial statements have been classified, described and disclosed properly.

SO WHAT MAKES UP AN ACCOUNTING SYSTEM?

An entity. The business entity must be identified, and defined as to type (such as service, retail, or manufacturing). The accounting system must focus on the entity and include transactions that are only the entity's. Even if you are a sole proprietor, the accounting information should not include any personal transactions. It can be tempting for owners to include personal expenses with their company expenses to reduce company taxes. However not only is this fraud against the tax authorities, it also misrepresents the results of the company's operations. Occasionally the company will have legitimate transactions with its owners. In these instances the transactions should be clearly accounted for separately so as to be identified as "related party."

Business activities. If you think of a company as an entity, your accounting system must identify, record, and report on transactions between your company and outside persons or entities. This includes transactions such as your sales, purchases, and borrowings. Your accounting must also identify in-company transactions, such as wages to employees and transfers between departments or locations.

Policies and procedures. You probably know you need "books and records." Maintaining a checkbook, while a part of an accounting system, is not enough even if your company is so small that you are its only employee, have no assets other than one checking account, have no debt other than to vendors for goods or services, and account for your activities on a cash basis. Today, what accountants refer to as "the company books" are more likely to be the output from accounting software packages in either print or electronic format. But even software alone is not enough.

An accounting system must also include policies and procedures to help insure that the information reported by the system is reliable and to help prevent employee theft. (Remember the 6%?) These policies and procedures are often referred to as a system of internal controls. Such a system will provide assurance to you (and your auditor) about the accuracy of the amounts recorded and help identify errors and omissions. It discourages employee theft and helps protect assets. The accounting system gives the owner controls over the flow of dollars in and out of the company. It will also standardize good management practices and procedures so that no matter which employee performs a task or transaction it will be done and recorded in the same way.

TELL ME A BIT MORE ABOUT INTERNAL CONTROLS

Components of internal controls include the environment within your business; assessing the risk of error, omissions, and theft; establishing control procedures; communicating the procedures; and monitoring the system to insure that it works. Environment generally refers to the integrity with which the owners and managers run the business. If the owners steal, the employees will too. End of story.

Common control procedures include segregation of duties, reconciliation of bank accounts, documentation, controlling access to assets, and knowing your employees. Segregation of duties requires that persons handling assets such as cash, inventory, and receivables are not also responsible for recording the transactions that affect those assets. In a small business, segregation of duties can be difficult due to the small number of employees. In these cases, the owner can be included as part of the accounting system to provide additional segregation.

Documentation means to have information that supports the transaction and to have the transaction authorized. As an owner, don't sign blank checks. When asked to sign checks, look at supporting documents. Allow your employees to shift money between bank accounts only after you authorize them to do so. Add new vendors or employees to the accounting system only after they are authorized and verified.

Know your employees so that you are aware of any changes in their behavior or lifestyle. Do any of them have a substance abuse problem? You should always check references before hiring a new employee. Finally, encourage your employees to speak up if they see anything that makes them uncomfortable or suspicious.

Safeguarding assets includes depositing cash, checks, and charges daily, and locking up blank checks or check stock. Also important is providing password restrictions to computer systems and programs, changing passwords regularly, backing up the system daily, maintaining lists of equipment, controlling access to important identification numbers or account numbers, and obtaining and maintaining insurance coverage.

WHAT DO I NEED TO DO TO SET UP MY ACCOUNTING SYSTEM?

Of course, most business owners have some sort of accounting system or computer program. Many businesses are run from either the personal or business version of QuickBooks Payroll. If you have no employees and make less than $50,000, such a basic program might be adequate. But if you ever expect to expand the business, sell it, or take in partners, you'll want a more complete system.

To set up your accounting system we recommend that you first check resources in your industry. Most industries have associations that are a good source of information about critical operating statistics, typical accounting and reporting issues, and areas of possible employee theft. Next you should talk to an accountant at length about an accounting system that would be cost effective for the size and type of business that you currently have and that could grow with your company. Among other items, the agenda for this meeting should include choice of fiscal year, basis of accounting (cash or accrual), possible hardware and software choices, chart of accounts, types and timing of reports for your use and, of course, important internal controls that you should develop.

GOOD ACCOUNTING RECORDS RESULT IN A TAX AUDIT WITH NO CHANGES

A construction company was selected for a tax audit. During the year that was selected for audit, the owner of the company had built a residence for his family. This raised red flags with the tax agent. Further, the owner ran the transaction through the company's job accounting system in order to keep good track of his expenses. Fortunately, he insisted that the entire home construction be segregated into special accounts set up for the purpose. All of the accounts were labeled with the name of his home and were easily identifiable. The tax agent requested and received from the controller all of the details and documentation for these accounts. Upon examining the information the agent was satisfied that the expenses to construct the home had not been included in the company's expenses deducted on the tax return. The excellent controls in the accounting system clearly identified which expenses were for the home and segregated those expenses in the records. The agent completed the audit with no changes to the tax return.

LACK OF ACCOUNTING RECORDS RESULTS IN A FAILED SALE OF A BUSINESS

ABC Company was interested in acquiring a small family-owned and-operated business that provided specialized services and was offered for sale. ABC did not perform these services and was interested in acquiring the expertise and offering the services to their existing customers. ABC's management met a number of times with the family. Both sides had agreed upon a number of issues that included employment of the family selling the business.

The family was asking $275,000 for their company, but was slow in providing accounting information. Finally they submitted three years of income tax returns. ABC sought the advice of their accountant regarding the sales price. The family reported the company as a sole proprietorship on a Schedule C in the husband and wife's personal income tax return. Only one of the returns had a small profit, the other years showed losses. Upon comparing the expenses over the three years presented, it appeared highly likely that personal expenses had been included with the business expenses. Furthermore the expenses shown on the tax return varied considerably from year to year. The accountant requested additional accounting information but the family was unable to provide any. Consequently ABC Company offered $150,000 for the business, but the family wasn't willing to sell at that price. Four years later the family is still operating the company and has not been able to sell it. The failure of this sale was entirely caused by a lack of accurate accounting records.

CONCLUSION

A good accounting system is the basis for documenting your business for others and gathering management information for yourself. Unless a business is tiny and the number of transactions minimal, few would argue with the value of a good accounting system. Helping you implement — or change to — the right system is the first thing your accountant can do for you. Once that's in place you have increased flexibility and control to manage your business profitably.

QUESTIONS TO ASK YOURSELF

1. Am I satisfied with my current accounting system?

2. Can I get daily, weekly, and monthly reports from my system?

3. Does my accounting system produce information that is useful for my decision making?

4. Would I be prepared if I were to be audited next week?

5. Do I have systems to uncover and eliminate employee theft?

6. Is proprietary information protected?

QUESTIONS TO ASK YOUR ACCOUNTANT

1. Have you set up accounting systems for businesses like mine?

2. What type of accounting system would be cost effective now and could grow with my business?

3. Would operating on a cash or accrual basis be best for my business?

4. What fiscal year would you recommend my business use?

5. What financial reports would be most useful for me?

6. What internal controls would you recommend for my business?

7. How do you help me if I'm audited?

CHAPTER 3

Your Family Business History:
Past and Future

Most good accountants and other professional business advisors will have at least a rudimentary understanding of your industry, but they will likely want to know more about the specifics of your particular business. By understanding what has occurred in the past, your professional advisors can more easily help you chart your future course.

Your starting point in a new relationship with any professional advisor is to provide a business history or company overview. Your advisors will sit with you and briefly chart changes in the business and profitability over time. They will likely ask you about your original motivation for starting the business, your greatest obstacles and concerns, and your key milestones along the way. Early in the life of a business, the story is usually about finding the right mix of products and services, and achieving growth. Along the way there might be technology changes, acquisitions, family members coming into the business, and more.

YOUR TRUSTED BUSINESS ADVISOR

While people sometimes think that accountants are only skilled at addressing financial issues, in fact the highest-value use of your accountant is to involve him or her almost as a member of your team. While we do our best to remain impartial sounding boards for your business, we find it beneficial to work with you over time to understand your business from the inside, as well. As professional advisors, we have worked closely with a wide variety of businesses over the years and we can offer an objective perspective on issues as diverse as human dynamics and new products. Sometimes we can see the proverbial forest more clearly while you may be distracted by day-to-day management issues.

It is in your best interest to help your professional advisor understand your goals for your business. Knowing where you want to be in five years can be important when making decisions on a daily basis from both a financial and strategic point of view. We can help with business planning on a number of dimensions. For instance, your accountant is trained in certain business methodologies like the SWOT analysis taught in business schools for decades. Looking at your Strengths, Weaknesses, Opportunities, and Threats from an outside perspective can often help you decide how to use your strengths better to take advantage of opportunities in your industry. Or from a competitive perspective, you may be able to anticipate threats or exploit the weaknesses of your competitors to find new niches or expand markets.

Unfortunately, many family businesses only think to call their accountant in as a business advisor when they are in crisis mode or face management transitions. And, of course, transitions in family businesses are often seen as fraught with peril. After all, the statistics say that most businesses won't make the transition to a second generation of family management. (*Forbes* magazine recently said that only 30% of businesses do.) For this reason, your accountant can be most valuable to the family business as a long-term trusted advisor. There are many issues that we can help with, long before or after a transition is at issue.

THE HUMAN FACTOR

Despite the stereotypical portrayal of accountants as "number crunchers," many human factors impact the success of your business operations, so naturally we consider them in our general consulting. It may sound odd, but an accountant can act almost serve as a therapist in some situations. As the owner or senior manager of a business, there are some issues you just can't discuss with employees, competitors, or even family members. An accountant who understands your business can act as a sounding board and advisor.

FAMILY ROLES VS. BUSINESS ROLES

Running a business is a daunting task. And family businesses have their own set of unique issues and dynamics. Many of the issues that family businesses face occur because of the confusion between family roles and business roles. For instance, in a family business, the roles can differ greatly from the traditional roles within the family unit. In a family, the oldest child has a clear role, as does the youngest, and so on. But in the business, the oldest may not necessarily be the boss-in-training. The oldest may fit better in a finance or sales capacity while a younger sibling may possess the qualities of a good candidate for the leadership role. And then there are sons-in-law, daughters-in-law, cousins, aunts, uncles, and other relatives. How do *they* fit into the family and business dynamics?

When some family members work in the business and some don't, it can become even more complicated. For instance, family members working in the business may receive higher salaries and better perks than they would receive in the job market. This can cause resentment from family members not involved in the business — and from non-related employees of the business. Sometimes these issues only surface when the business is passed on to heirs. But the solution in either case is to keep a clear distinction between the role of owners and the role of employees. If you work in the business, you should draw a salary that you would earn in a similar business. If the business distributes profits and you own a share in it, then you are entitled to an owner's dividend as well. But family workers in the business are not entitled to "milk" the business to the detriment of outside family owners.

YOUR BUSINESS HISTORY: PAST, PRESENT, AND FUTURE

As mentioned earlier, an effective professional advisor applies their knowledge of your business's history to help you achieve your future goals and objectives. Often the variables that were significant in the past for your business success will continue to be important in the future as well. But the future will also bring new variables as conditions change in both your industry and your family.

Passing Your Business On

One of the future business issues covered in other chapters is succession. It's worth mentioning here that when you plan your future, succession is a major event that must be considered. If you do not plan for this process well in advance, you'll be at a great disadvantage. After all, as the old saying goes, if you fail to plan, you're planning to fail.

There are only four ways you can make a transition out of your business: (a) die, (b) go public, (c) sell to outsiders, and (d) sell to family or employees. We can't do anything about the first case. However, dying without a succession plan is like dying without a will — it can only cause problems for those who survive you. We won't cover going public and selling to outsiders here. We'll focus briefly on transitioning the business to family members.

Years of experience have taught us that entrepreneurs usually have a difficult time relinquishing control — of anything. Many people who start businesses don't make an easy transition to managing their own businesses. The entrepreneurial personality is different from the managerial personality. However, you've built a successful business, so you've learned some middle ground.

The same issues are in play when considering your succession or retirement. Some people dread even the thought of retirement while others take to it immediately. However, there is a middle ground between giving up *all* control and retiring "down south" that can also help with succession. In many public corporations, the former president or CEO becomes Chairman of the Board. This allows the company to tap into your experience — and you to maintain some control of the company — while giving a new CEO a bit of room to "stretch their wings."

As Chair, you can selectively choose business projects that are of interest to you, but which you never had time to get around to while running the business. This can be a high-value activity in any organization. When you're busy running a business, often you don't have the time or focus to step back and look at the big picture. Having the time to finally drain the swamp instead of fighting alligators can be a very valuable benefit to the business. By focusing primarily on special projects, you can contribute to the business, be available as a consultant, protect your own interests, and enjoy a flexible schedule.

EXAMPLES OF TRANSITIONS

A fairly typical family situation illustrates several of these points. The founder of a mid-sized manufacturing business had a brother and a daughter who were both involved in the business. He also had two sons who were not interested in joining the family business. Over the years, the founder did not make it clear who would succeed him or what each person would inherit and the daughter assumed that she would be overlooked when the business was transitioned in the future.

When the founder finally faced the issue of succession and discussed it with his family, he announced that he would like his daughter to assume the role of the next CEO. The founder's brother made it clear that he was happiest as a CFO and was not interested in becoming CEO. The founder was not ready to leave the business altogether, so he found a niche area to explore, which he'd had no time to pursue when he was CEO. Once all the parties were clear on their roles, they spent over five years transitioning successfully.

One of the sons who was not involved in the business was an artist and needed financial support. All the children were to receive equal ownership. By clarifying the separation between ownership and control, dividends were paid to all the children, independent of whether they worked in the business or not. (Those who worked also received salaries, of course.) By opening the lines of communication and clarifying the roles of each family member, the transition went smoothly and, as a bonus, the business expanded in the new niche profitably.

On the contrary, a lot can go wrong when a good plan and communication are not established, as illustrated by the case of another manufacturing business. Again, the business was founded by the father who built it up over a length of time spanning nearly three decades. His three sons worked in the business all their lives. They started on the loading dock as teenagers and worked their way up, through the different areas of the business.

The business eventually went public but the family maintained control. Sadly, the father died suddenly — without a succession plan. There was no plan for resolving disputes and there were no strong, impartial, outside advisors. The three sons had equal ownership and poor communication. They argued over every decision to be made. The business manufactured high-tech stereo equipment and the market was changing fast. Technology and outsourcing decisions were among many that didn't get made on time. They lost market share and profitability. Because the business had always been profitable, the brothers had enjoyed luxury lifestyles that they weren't willing to give up. Within ten years the business foundered and it was sold out from under them.

Some of the differences between the two cases are obvious and widely applicable. Some will vary depending on your situation. Most family businesses don't survive to the second generation. If you want to be on the positive side of that divide, plan your transition ahead of time.

CONCLUSION

No matter how effective you are at running your business, you need trusted business advisors who can offer outside expertise and perspective. And when you pass on the business, your successors may need even more help in order to make a smooth transition. An effective and respected outside advisor not only offers a different perspective and can help with decisions, but can act as a counterbalance and deal with the difficult family issues that must be addressed.

Although accountants are not "real" therapists, they should be aware of family dynamics in order to help you reach your goals, taking into account the numbers, the management information derived from the numbers, and the human elements needed to make a business successful for years to come.

QUESTIONS TO ASK YOURSELF

1. Do I have a transition plan and, if so, does my family know about it?

2. When will I be willing to give up some or all control?

3. Am I comfortable that others have the ability to run my company?

4. Have I arranged for family members to receive necessary training in the business?

5. Should I involve a non-family manager as a transition or to help the family?

6. Are there business projects that I'd like to work on if I had time?

7. Are there new areas where I could develop the business?

QUESTIONS TO ASK YOUR ACCOUNTANT

1. What is your experience with businesses like mine?

2. What is your experience with family businesses?

3. How have you helped your clients with the management transition process?

4. What does your role as a professional advisor encompass?

5. How can you help us be more successful now and in the future?

CHAPTER 4

What Form of Business Should I Use?

Most readers will have already chosen a legal form to do business under. If you haven't, then by default you are probably operating as a "sole proprietor." This chapter will serve as a brief overview of the common forms of business available to you. After reading it, you may want to change your form of business. In that case you should consult with your attorney as well as your accountant for the details of liability and tax considerations. Some of the more common forms of business entities are as follows:

SOLE PROPRIETORSHIPS

A sole proprietorship is available for those business owners who will own 100% of the business. A sole proprietorship is probably the easiest and least expensive form of entity to establish but may also be the least efficient in liability protection considerations and possibly income tax considerations. You are liable for the business and income from it is taxed as part of your overall personal income.

PARTNERSHIPS

Partnerships are available where there are going to be two or more owners of the business. Most partnerships are general partnerships where you are all liable for what the others do in the name of the business.

Limited partnerships have a general partner who assumes the liability and has control, and limited partners who usually put up the money and have "limited" liability. Many investment partnerships are in this form. If you're in business with a friend, you are general partners. You should have a clear partnership agreement. Partnerships can work well if handling disagreements and buyouts are considered at the beginning.

CORPORATIONS

A corporation is available whether there is one owner or a number of owners. A corporation attempts to provide a shield for the owners from liability that originates inside the corporation. Depending on the type of corporation that is selected, the owners may pay tax on the corporate income or the corporation may pay tax on its income. If the corporation is paying tax on its income, the treatment of certain income items and the tax rates that apply to them may differ significantly from the tax treatment and tax rates applicable to the same income in a sole proprietorship.

LIMITED LIABILITY COMPANIES

In the overall scheme of business, the limited liability company is among the newer types of entities that may be available. Limited liability companies possess some of the characteristics of corporations, while at the same time possessing some of the characteristics of partnerships or sole proprietorships. They, too, are available whether there is one owner or numerous owners.

Other forms that may be used for businesses include trusts, cooperatives, and numerous variations of the entities discussed above.

SELECTING YOUR FORM OF BUSINESS

The selection of a business entity involves numerous factors. Among those things that should be considered by any potential business owner are the following:

- Ease of formation
- Cost of formation
- Ownership, both present and future
- Management

- Liability protection
- Funding
- State or provincial, local, and federal tax considerations
- Succession plan
- Type of business
- Location of business

The selection of a business entity will typically result in numerous trade-offs between the factors to be considered. Where one entity might have the most favorable tax implications, the same entity may have the least favorable liability protection characteristics. Where one entity may be appropriate if the business owner anticipates that the business will be carried on for several generations in the future, another type of entity may be appropriate if that same business owner anticipates operating the business only during his or her career and then liquidating the business and retiring on the proceeds from the sale of the business.

Chapters longer than this one can easily be written about each of the above considerations. Unless potential business owners are knowledgeable about all of the types of entities and the impact of the above considerations on each type of entity, they should consult with their attorney and accountant concerning the appropriate entity for their business.

Obviously, there is no entity that is perfect for every situation. The proper selection of an entity is critical at the outset of a business. However, the choice of entity should be reviewed periodically. For instance, you may start a small business to test an idea and do it as a sole proprietor. If it looks like it will grow and be profitable, you may change to a corporation. In many cases, changes in tax laws, family situations, the nature of the business, and numerous other factors may result in the entity that was appropriate at the outset of the business no longer being appropriate. In some cases, the timing on changing the form of entity that is being used may be critical.

WHAT IF YOU MAKE A MISTAKE?

So what happens if the wrong choice of entity is made? A couple of real-life examples can illustrate the answer to this question. The first example is one concerning a business owner who had operated as a corporation for approximately 40 years. This business owner had a very successful business and continually realized large profits. His accountant did a year-end review of his financial statements on an annual basis. As a follow-up to this review, a general planning meeting was held between the business owner, the managers of the business, and the accountant to discuss any changes that had been made in the operation of the business and any changes outside the business that the business owner should be aware of. One year, as a result of this planning meeting, the owner's accountant advised him of a change in the state law that would be very costly to his corporation. As a result of this advice, the business owner was able to convert his form of business from a corporation to a limited partnership for state law purposes and thereby avoid approximately $50,000 per year in state franchise taxes.

The second business owner was not quite so fortunate. In this case, the business owner left a position in an organization to start his own business rather early in his career life. Having previously been in a role that made him somewhat knowledgeable of business entities, he chose to form a corporation and in fact formed it without any professional assistance. While the corporate form of business served him fairly well for a number of years, changes in the types of assets that the business owned, as well as changes in federal tax laws, made the corporation the least desirable form of business at a later point in time.

For personal reasons, this business owner decided to sell the assets that the corporation owned, liquidate the corporation, and retire on the proceeds from such liquidation. He had heard much talk that the federal income tax rates on long-term capital gains had been lowered to 15%. Based on this tax rate, he negotiated a sale of the assets of the business. In making such a sale, he essentially determined how much money he thought he needed to retire and used this as a starting point for backing into the sales price, allowing for a 15% tax on the proceeds from the sale.

Imagine his frustration and displeasure when he was informed at the end of the year that the capital gains rates did not apply to his corporation. Thus, where he had anticipated a 15% tax rate, the actual tax rate was 34%. To add insult to injury, he also learned that there would be a 15% tax rate that would apply to the value of all the assets of the corporation as they were distributed to him in liquidation of the corporation. When all was said and done, the effective combined state and federal tax rate that was applied to the sale of the assets was approximately 49%, rather than the 15% that the taxpayer had anticipated. This case not only illustrates the need to monitor your entity selection, but it also illustrates the need to maintain ongoing relationships with competent professionals.

CONCLUSION

If you haven't chosen a business form, use the questions below to understand the issues you'll want to consider or ask your accountant about. If you are already operating under a form of business, talk to your accountant about tax implications of other possible forms. Be sure to consider future profit patterns and estate issues. For instance, traditional corporations can keep money in the business without taxes to the owners. And the right business form, such as a *trust,* may lower your estate taxes. Like many of the management and accounting details involved with business, your form of business can be important to you.

QUESTIONS TO ASK YOURSELF

1. Am I happy with my current business entity?

2. If I have a partnership, do I have a clear buyout agreement?

3. If I have a partnership, how do we handle the death of a partner?

4. Do I want to change my legal form of business?

QUESTIONS TO ASK YOUR ACCOUNTANT

1. Do you think my current form of business is the right one for me?

2. What would be the advantages of changing to another form of business?

3. Can you recommend attorneys expert on this issue?

4. Would a trust offer me more protection?

CHAPTER 5

Business Process Documentation: Key People and Processes

At the start of a business, and most often for many years into its existence, operations are dominated by one, two, or three individuals who maintain vital information about the business in their heads. Operational processes and procedures are not documented and preserved. This means that in case of emergencies, no one in the organization can pick up the pieces and move on quickly and easily.

Businesses cite many reasons for not writing procedures down. These reasons include time pressures, that people performing the tasks may complete them in different ways, key people wanting to remain essential, and simple inertia or laziness. Documentation isn't seen as important until it is too late — as George in the following example found out.

George arrived at his office on Monday morning at the same time he had arrived for the past ten years. However this morning his office manager was not there, as she had always been for years. Instead there was a message in his voicemail from her daughter indicating that Margaret had been injured in an automobile accident over the weekend and was hospitalized in critical condition. Her recovery was uncertain at best.

George panicked. Margaret was the go-to person for all of his business operations. She was a partner in all but name. They had made a good team. While George was on the road selling and dealing with customer service issues, Margaret dealt with all other aspects of the business. After speaking with Bert, Margaret's assistant, it became clear that George had a problem. Only Margaret was aware of critical phases of the business operations, key files, and so on, and she was not able to speak or provide instructions. The business came to a near standstill. Several customers got upset when previously placed orders weren't followed up on. Revenues dropped because, instead of selling, George had to spend time figuring out what needed to be done and placating unhappy customers. It took weeks to sort things out so that other people could step in and do Margaret's work.

CREATING YOUR DOCUMENTATION

To begin the process of documenting the procedures used every day by your business, first determine which processes are vital to your organization. They may include some or all of the following:

- Marketing and sales
- Contracting with customers
- Production of your product or service
- Purchasing materials or goods used in providing your service or production of your product
- Invoicing and collection procedures
- Personnel training and review

Next, assemble a team of people within your organization who regularly perform the tasks under each broad category. For example, if you are setting out to document the customer contracting process, the team should include a salesperson, the administrative person who prepares proposals, and a production person who would fulfill customer orders. The purpose of the meeting is not only to discuss the process, but also to document it from beginning to end. At the end of the meeting each member of the team will leave with a rough draft of the process that they can subsequently edit and finalize. Final process documentation should include all internal forms used in the process as well as work instructions, if any, related to the steps within the process.

USE YOUR OWN STYLE

Your documentation can take many different forms. Some businesses will utilize flowcharts that depict decisions, procedures, and forms. Others will use written steps that are essentially the same as a flowchart, except they are written. Still others will use a combination of flowcharts, written instructions, and forms. The style of documentation is important only from the standpoint of its usefulness to your staff and for training.

Once the process is complete, you cannot stuff the final process book in a drawer and breathe a sigh of relief. The process book or manual needs to become a vital, living part of your organization. It can serve as more than documentation. It can be a catalyst to discuss how things are done and how they can be improved. Over time your processes and procedures will change due to new regulations, customer requests, employee suggestions, or new lines of business. As these changes occur, the manual needs to be updated so that it is current. Otherwise you will be in the same situation that George found himself in.

Many organizations hire a consultant to help them document their processes. As mentioned earlier, every business needs to service its customers first and therefore administrative functions tend to take a back burner. A consultant can keep the process moving by setting interim deadlines and goals, leading team discussions, and documenting the processes during the team discussions.

CONCLUSION

Documenting your processes and procedures is not an exciting task for most entrepreneurial founders. If you already have good documentation in place, you may be able to implement improvements fairly easily by delegating responsibility to each division. If you have to start from scratch, try to get a rough draft done by "talking out" what you and other key personnel do. Or interview each of them — or the last person they trained — on how they do their jobs. You'll be better off with documentation, so start where you are and move forward now.

QUESTIONS TO ASK YOURSELF

1. Do you have one, two, or three key people who hold vital business operating practices in their heads?

2. Are you ready to move the organization from a free-flow method of operating to controlled operations where

personnel are expected to follow documented processes or offer suggestions for better alternatives?

3. Do you find that your personnel have divergent methods of achieving the same end result with some methods more efficient than others?

4. Do you want better job descriptions for new employees?

5. Do you spend a great deal of time training organization personnel in business operations?

6. Are you in an industry where obtaining your ISO registration would provide additional business opportunities for you?

7. Do you want to eliminate redundant processes, but are uncertain what the impact would be?

8. Are you ready to commit resources to the project? (What is the budget for the project in dollars, time, and internal resources?)

9. Do you want to hire a consultant to monitor and assist in the project?

10. What format should the final documentation take?

QUESTIONS TO ASK YOUR ACCOUNTANT

1. What experience do you have in documentation of processes?

2. Can you provide suggested industry practices?

3. What is your estimated timeline for the project?

4. What is the estimated cost of the project?

5. What format will the documentation take (for example, flowchart, written paragraphs, or a combination)?

6. Are you open to alternative documentation formats if we would prefer a format different from your suggested format?

7. What training will our personnel need to have to make future changes to the documented processes?

8. What is your follow-up plan?

9. Once the processes are documented, can you suggest methods of measuring the efficiency or effectiveness of the processes to achieve desired results?

CHAPTER 6

Strategic Planning and Competition

Plans are nothing; planning is everything.
DWIGHT D. EISENHOWER

The goal of strategic planning is to help you make the best possible management decisions for your business. Nobody will disagree with that goal, yet few business owners implement their strategic plan. Much has been written and discussed about the subject of strategic planning from every conceivable vantage point by college professors, industry experts, well-meaning consultants, and self-touted gurus. Unfortunately, even when they develop a strategic plan, most business owners fail to follow through with implementation, missing the opportunity to realize the benefits of strategic planning.

In advising clients, we believe that *the results* of the planning process, not the plan itself, hold the key to your success. Strategic planning, in its most effective form, provides business owners and management with a framework for decision making and resource allocation. This leads to clarity of purpose and the achievement of competitive advantage.

In order to remain competitive, you must think and plan strategically. Global competition, combined with diminished and restricted resources, makes it critical for business owners to constantly analyze the market and determine the status of their businesses. The ability of owners and managers to develop and articulate a clear vision, along with the ability to implement specific goals and objectives, goes a long way toward determining the success of a business.

An alternative to strategic planning is subscribing to the management theory of Christopher Columbus:

- When he departed, he did not know where he was headed.
- When he arrived, he had no idea where he was.
- When he returned, he could not say where he had been!

To be successful, you must know where you are headed and how to get there. Your planning is your blueprint for success in your business. Great businesses are built on solid foundations. Great strategists know how they intend to compete in their marketplaces. Those who understand the principles of business strategy make superior decisions. It's that simple.

Today, your competition is far less obvious and predictable. Due to dramatic changes in the global economy, your competition has become more difficult to monitor, understand, anticipate, and contest. Adding to these difficulties, businesses are now faced with nontraditional competitors that include any person, place, or thing that can potentially take their customers' dollars. Competitors may now be viewed not only as opposing companies within an industry, but also as alternative ways for buyers to obtain desired results.

IMPLEMENTING YOUR STRATEGY

Regardless of how it is defined, strategy is first and foremost about making and implementing decisions. These decisions will determine the shape, form, and ultimate outcome of your business. Consequently, the intent of a strategic plan is to shape the future of your company.

The power of an idea is in its implementation. The strategic planning process is driven by analysis, decisions, and action. Thus, proper planning ensures that the overall desired purpose of your company will be achieved effectively and efficiently.

Strategic planning is *not* about creating a plan that sits on the shelf only to be dusted off and replaced annually or every few years when the process is repeated. In order to be effective, a strategic plan must be dynamic and must be carried out.

Often owners and managers of closely held or family-owned businesses think of strategy as relevant only to large corporations. Nothing could be farther from the truth! All big businesses started out small. Most were little more than an idea — a vision — in the mind of their founders.

Is there a business owner anywhere who does not want to increase the profitability of their business, create more discretionary time, and achieve a higher quality of life for themselves and their families?

DEVELOPING YOUR STRATEGIC PLAN

As mentioned in other chapters, the key to creating value in your business is to spend more time working *on* your business, and less time working *in* it. Your focus should be on *managing* the business, not simply *working* in it. By focusing on the management of your business and positioning the business to excel in the marketplace, you will maximize the return on your money and time. A well-formulated strategic planning program is designed to help you achieve this maximization.

A simple yet revealing way to begin the strategic planning process is to ask yourself a critical question: What needs to happen over the next three to five years in my business for me to be pleased with its progress and meet my goals? Forget what you have to do to make your business work. What do you want your business to do for you?

WHAT A PLAN DOES

Initially, a strategic plan should serve to identify core business strengths and weaknesses, identify opportunities to exploit, develop or revisit your company's vision, and design or refine the mission statement. The result should provide the answers to three key questions.

- Where is the business now?
- Where do I want it to be?
- What needs to be done to get it there?

Your strategic planning process should provide the framework to set measurable targets and create an agenda for action. You should define and articulate a business strategy and work with customers to identify key frustrations with the business. You should gather insights from managers and team members, develop a customer service strategy to enhance quality of service and customer loyalty, and review and improve operating procedures. You may need to alter the business's organizational structure to coincide with the new strategy. You will definitely need to develop a marketing plan to gain and selectively acquire the right type of new customers. Finally, you should pull everything together in a management control plan that assures continued progress. In short, a good plan should make your business more profitable *and* easier to run.

A comprehensive strategic plan systematically and continuously addresses each of the major components of your business, including team members, products and services, customers, suppliers, competitors, financial systems, and market trends. Since each of these components is intricately connected, success or failure of one will serve to strengthen or weaken each of the others.

IMPLEMENTING YOUR PLAN

Once a strategy is defined, owners and managers should focus and invest resources on communicating, articulating, and reinforcing the vision to the business's team members. By constantly seeking to improve the effectiveness of the business, everyone involved can collectively work together to achieve greater success for themselves and the business.

Monitoring, follow through, and accountability are crucial in undertaking any initiative for change in your organization. Without them you risk ending up right back where you began. A modern definition of insanity is repeatedly engaging in the same behavior while expecting different results.

Unless you or a member of your management team is adept at strategic planning, working with an experienced, qualified professional is important. Such a professional can facilitate, leverage, and probably accelerate the process, yielding early benefits, particularly if your organization is new to the strategic planning process.

DOING IT RIGHT

PrepareNow Corporation, a distributor of aerospace parts, has been in business for over twenty years. Up until seven years ago it had marginal success, provided a mediocre income for the three owners, and less than competitive salaries for the team members. In essence, the business reached a performance plateau in revenue, products, and services that proved to be formidable. Driven by the challenge to improve and grow their business, the owners sought out and hired independent professionals for advice. They interviewed and selected a firm with the proper credentials and expertise to reach their objective. Seeking to clarify their personal and business goals, the owners came away from the initial planning retreat with a renewed and focused vision and mission statement for the company.

Their efforts yielded results just short of amazing. Now, regularly pursued with inquiries and offers about potentially merging or selling their business, they have a solid idea of the business's value and the knowledge of viable options for an exit strategy. For now, they decided to look for acquisition candidates of their own as a means to gain economies of scale, improve margins, and enter new markets. After having acquired several companies in markets diverse from theirs and a few others that complemented their current product lines, the size of the company quadrupled.

While never ignoring their business, the owners can and do take time away to plan continuing strategy and for physical, mental, and emotional rejuvenation. They spend more quality time with their families while feeling confident they have done everything within their control to maximize the value of the business, their personal wealth, and their families' futures.

NOT DOING IT

EndlessCycle Corporation, a manufacturer of equipment parts, is owned by John Brown. John founded the business ten years ago, after a 15-year career as a product engineer. He worked hard to build the business to provide him and his family with an adequate income. They were comfortable although they never seemed to have the ability to create any real wealth inside the business or as a family unit. John never saw a need to work *on* his business. He enjoyed micromanaging every aspect of what the business did. For John, hiring another manager to create time for John to think about growing his business and increasing profits only meant he would have to take a pay cut. John felt the idea of hiring someone from the outside to analyze his business was out of the question. This is his job, he thought. He didn't need help with it.

John's kids were growing up and he never seemed to have the time to take his wife and family on a vacation. John, concerned about his health, suppressed any thoughts of having a health issue that would take him away from his business for an extended period of time. Still waiting for something to miraculously occur to propel the business to the next level, he continues to operate in the same manner as he did when he founded the business. He's still in business so he figures he must be doing something right, but why are his needs not met? Without a plan, his efforts have not produced what he wants and needs.

CONCLUSION

Many business owners don't think strategic planning is important to their success. In fact, the right plan can help you improve your business and reach your personal goals more easily. Done right, it can give you new insights and directions for your business. If your business is not where you want it to be and you are not comfortable doing strategic planning on your own, get help. The right input can be very cost effective, as well as change your business for the better.

QUESTIONS TO ASK YOURSELF

1. What is the purpose of my business?

2. What do I want my business to accomplish?

3. Has my business lived up to my expectations?

4. Are the vision and mission statements for my business clearly documented?

5. Does my strategic plan develop the short-term, mid-range, and long-term objectives of my business?

6. Am I satisfied with the way my business is currently progressing?

7. Do I take specific time each month to review the progress of my company?

8. Do I have adequate systems and processes in place to measure the progress of my business?

9. What would happen to my business if I were to take a six-month vacation?

10. Is my accountant proactive in discussing the future plans and strategies of my business instead of always focusing on historical events and data?

11. Does my accountant offer new insights or challenge the validity of ideas and concepts I discuss about my business's direction, initiatives, and strategy?

QUESTIONS TO ASK YOUR ACCOUNTANT

1. What type of experience do you have in the area of strategic planning with businesses of my size and in my industry?

2   During your career, how many client strategic planning engagements have you been involved in?

3. Have you ever facilitated a strategic planning session for one of your clients?

4. How can you help me grow and increase the value of my business?

5. Do you offer services that assist with vision and mission statement development?

6. What kind of products and services can you offer to provide assistance with team building?

7. Can you provide assistance with developing a customer service strategy?

8. How would I develop an optimal marketing plan for my business?

9. Should I grow my business internally or by acquisition?

10. How can I be sure I have the most effective business organizational structure?

11. Do you offer a program that establishes formal or informal measures to tell me how my business is performing?

CHAPTER 7

Why Budgeting and Planning
Are Important

Budgeting and planning just might be the most important tasks of managing a business. Indeed, it is probably not an overstatement to say that a budget is the foundation of running your business. Budgeting is as important to your business as diet is to the human body.

Many of us can relate budgets and planning to a diet. Usually your physician will recommend that you need to go on a diet for health reasons. In the financial world your accountant may recommend that your business needs to go on a diet.

TYPES OF BUDGETING

There are two types of dieters or budgeters: those who say I'm going to lose weight by "eating better" and those who get serious and actually count their calorie intake and monitor their exercise. Those who choose the path of just "eating better" or "planning to make more money" usually end up right where they were, or worse. They're frequently bewildered at how they arrived in their present state, and are left wondering how they gained so many pounds and lost so much money this year.

The second type of budgeter takes the extra effort to examine both the expenses and revenue cycles and the company's assets and liabilities. This is a great opportunity to identify those areas that have been overlooked in the past, but are now looked at closely for budgeting purposes. There will, of course, be good months and bad months with your financial diet, but remember the budget is a tool that is continually working. With a budget you can identify when those "down" months are on the horizon and be better prepared to handle the cash flow issues that come with those special months.

A budget is essential for any business owner. There are many different ways to obtain the results that your company is striving for. The key is to find some time every week to work *on* your business, not just *in* it. A budget is the road map and plan for any business to chart their journey and reach their goals (and remember to always consult your "physician").

THE BUSINESS PLANNING CYCLE

A budget is part of an overall business planning cycle that consists of three components. First, the *strategic plan,* which considers the company's mission, vision, and plan for dealing with competition (see Chapter 6). Second, the *operational plan,* that includes a five-year plan tied to the *strategic plan* and incorporates goals for new product development, plant capacity, market expansion, and staffing requirements. Third is the *financial plan*, where your company projects financial statements, required cash flow, and financing needs.

Planning gives you a proactive approach — as opposed to a reactive approach — to your cash flow needs. This will save the company and you time and money. It will also help you sleep better at night knowing that a proactive approach is building value in your company.

YOUR PLANNING "DIET"

The following examples outline the importance of your financial diet.

Marcus started a manufacturing business in printing and retail sales right out of high school. He worked very hard in his business and for the most part had a successful company. However, as he got away for a long weekend, to celebrate his 30th high school reunion, he realized that he was working harder in the business, but he seemed to be falling further and further behind.

Not only was Marcus working harder, but the bank account was running out of funds before the month ran out of days! There were other things that didn't "feel" right either, but who had time to try to figure out what was going on with all of the things that needed to be done:

> Daily Sales Reports,
> Daily Supplier Orders, and
> Daily Receivable Calls.

> Weekly Payables to Pay,
> Weekly Payroll to Pay, and
> Weekly Payroll Tax Deposits.

> Monthly Sales Tax Reports,
> Monthly Bank Reconciliation, and
> Monthly Financial Statements.

> Quarterly Federal and State/Provincial Reports,
> Quarterly Sales Meetings, and
> Quarterly Meetings with the Banker.

> Annual Federal and State/Provincial Income Tax Returns,
> Annual Insurance Reviews, and
> Annual OSHA Visits.

Like many business owners, Marcus felt that he had no extra time to be proactive and to plan. But if Marcus would have taken the time to review, budget, and plan, he might have noticed:

- Margins have slowly deteriorated over the previous three years.
- Sales have been slowly falling over the last five years.
- His employee turnover is low compared to his competition; however, his labor cost is much higher.
- Inventory and receivables have grown during a time of declining sales.
- Account receivable collection times are progressively getting longer.

There are many other items that Marcus could react to if he only made the time to notice. Thankfully, Marcus still has time.

Marcus has a twin brother by the name of Mark who may be able to help Marcus out. Mark started a similar company across town after high school graduation. Mark, too, worked very hard *in* his business, but he also made time to work *on* his business.

Besides making sure that all of the compliance items were taken care of on a timely basis, Mark would find an extra hour or two a week to review the key indicators of his business. Mark realized that these key performance indicators could be different for every business and that they could change depending on the focus of the business during the current time period.

During this fiscal year, Mark was reviewing and focusing on the following seven key indicators for the company:

1. Daily and year-to-date sales compared to last year

2. Account receivable balances over 30 days and turnover ratios

3. Daily line of credit balance with the bank

4. Weekly production hours in the plant

5. Weekly back order of production jobs

6. Monthly financial statement budget variances

7. Quarterly employee turnover ratio compared to last year

Obviously, there could be many other indicators to review and act upon, but these seven are the ones that Mark felt were most informative about his company during the current year. By reviewing these items Mark is not only eliminating surprises, but he is also laying out and monitoring "the plan" for his business.

CONCLUSION

Budgeting and planning tend to be overlooked in the press of daily business. But like a healthy diet, proper planning can improve the health of your business. In the welter of financial information, often the most useful information gets lost. Your financial "doctor" should be able to help you measure and monitor the key financial and business information that will help you control your business, rather than it controlling you.

QUESTIONS TO ASK YOURSELF

1. Am I in control of my business?

2. Do I know my key financial indicators?

3. Do I have a written business plan?

4. Do I have a written budget?

5. Are my financial reports prompt enough to help me make management decisions?

QUESTIONS TO ASK YOUR ACCOUNTANT

1. Have you worked with businesses like mine?

2. What key financial indicators would you recommend that I measure regularly?

3. How can you help me with my planning and budgeting?

4. Can you help me get more timely financial information?

CHAPTER 8

Helping Your Managers Budget

...the budget process at most companies has to be the most ineffective process in management.
JACK WELCH,
famous for the successful management of GE

Many line managers hate budgeting. It is often looked at as a job they *have* to do that distracts them from their real jobs. As a result, budgets often take months to complete and are of little use for serious planning and goal setting. Managers — and sometimes owners — often look at budgeting as an annoyance or power struggle. One classic trick is for managers to simply add a factor to last year's budget and then use that figure to lobby for more money for their departments. Of course, this defeats the purpose of allotting capital efficiently. Recent studies have shown that on average 2–5% of total such budget items are padded.

The budgeting process is designed to help you plan for next year. At its best, it is an objective way to benchmark against yourself and allot capital and manpower in the business to the best purposes. However, in most companies it is an empty exercise that frustrates everyone involved. Some line managers simply have their administrative assistants do their budgets.

In a small company where the founder knows all the operations, budgeting is just a matter of getting the help you need to do accurate estimates and crunch the numbers. Even then, the founder is often not comfortable with budgeting and often doesn't get reports that give the information required to make better decisions in a timely fashion. In fact, the founder and other managers may not realize how useful the proper reports can be to their decision making. The right budgets and other financial documents can make your job easier and improve your business operations and profits.

If your company is big enough to delegate real responsibility to others, then the CEO can't know all the details. It becomes your job to provide policy guidance, new initiatives, inspiration, training, and oversight. As mentioned elsewhere, your job is to work *on* the business, more than *in* it.

WHY DO MANAGERS HATE BUDGETING?

Managers dislike budgeting for several reasons. First, it is another task added to their regular workload. It comes along every year, but is not a routine operation. Second, it is a task that they may not be comfortable doing. Surprisingly, some surveys show that the majority of managers are uncomfortable working with spreadsheets. While there are custom budgeting tools that are better than spreadsheets, most companies fall back on Excel-type tools. Third, many managers believe that corporate finance doesn't use their input anyway. Their numbers are often "adjusted" to fit what finance or top management wants. As one manager indicated, they impose the budget on us and then hold us responsible! Of course, this is a self-fulfilling prophecy because when managers are slow generating budget numbers, finance then has to do it. Fourth, the whole process tends to be adversarial. Central planning pushes for high goals to challenge divisions. Line management tries to scale goals back to add realism. And since bonuses tend to be set on how well managers hit their goals, lower goals are good for line management and higher goals are good for the corporation.

In one survey, less than half of line managers actually keyed in their projections themselves. And only about half provided explanations where budgets, or sections of budgets, weren't met (variances). Yet we know that when managers don't key in their own information, budgets are far less accurate. And when they don't learn from variances, the budget doesn't serve as a useful management tool so that improvements can be made every year.

These problems are not unique to family-owned businesses. The biggest businesses in the world, like Coca-Cola and Best Buy have faced these issues for years. For instance, even a division of Coke had a 52-page budgeting spreadsheet to deal with. Large companies have more resources to create a usable system than you do and it's still taken them years to set up better methods.

How Can You Get Managers More Involved?

Your finance department or your accountant should carry the ball to do the "number crunching" on your budget. But the key is to involve line managers. The front line knows more about sales projections, new product success, and client turnover than finance. They should be enlisted to make projections more realistic.

Tell your managers that you know they have the best first-hand knowledge of their areas. Ask them what customers want, what the problems in production are, and where opportunities lie for new sales and cost savings. Enlist their help in making the budget both accurate and challenging. And provide them the help they need to handle the mechanics of calculations.

If you have a computer (IT) department, it exists to serve management, not the other way around. Make sure you have people (or consultants) who know that their job is to support line managers, not create new reports for them to fill out.

A Budgeting Process

Even when everyone is involved in budgeting, oftentimes the final budgets are based more on guesswork and last year's numbers than on actual projections and estimates from all available knowledge. Budgeting should work backwards. Ideally, the budgeting process starts with sales. You forecast demand based on what existing customers say and on new income in the pipeline. These estimates then go to cost analysis. If you are a services firm, how many labor hours will be needed to fulfill demand? If you are a factory, what is your cost of materials needed to fulfill demand, and what are the overhead costs, right down to maintenance? Is corporate overhead the same as last year? What about new products or service initiatives?

Finance and your accountant can coordinate and support accurate budgeting. But if they act as good process consultants, they can also help you use your budget to create true change in your company.

The first thing your budgeting process needs to do is use numbers that are actually helpful to people in the field. Look for the numbers that predict your results, that give you early warnings. When you're simply setting your budget based on last year, you are locking yourself into your existing box. If you want to make serious changes in your business, you need to use a zero-based budget where every cost and income estimate is built from the ground up. That means it may be time to cut an old, unprofitable line that produces volume but no profits. Or it may be time to hire people in new areas to create new business.

If you give people targets adapted from last year, they will generally be able to meet them. But they will only be running in the same "hamster wheel" that they were last year. Starting your budget from scratch, and being willing to take real input from the front lines, is the best way to make your budget mean something to everyone. Instead of dreading the budget process, why not use it as an opportunity to move your company in the direction you want it to go?

WHY IS IT SO HARD?

When you have separate finance and operations (or service delivery) departments, you have a culture gap somewhat like that between engineering and sales. Each group thinks a different way and doesn't always respect the other. (Operation guys think finance guys just manipulate numbers without knowing what really goes on. The finance guys think front-line people don't communicate, don't understand the importance of our job, and give us bad data.)

Finance departments have a broader, more "yearly" view of operations. They are dealing with mandatory reports required by outside agencies. They are dealing with numbers summarized across a number of departments. And the department numbers they see are sometimes distorted or inaccurate for a variety of reasons. There is little incentive to produce timely reports that actually help front-line management.

Front-line managers are more project oriented within one aspect of the business. Late information is of little use to them and they don't see the irony of sometimes being the cause of the delay themselves. Their planning is typically short-term. They may think about return on investment of their projects, but they may not take general overhead into account.

TRAINING WORKS

One survey of larger companies showed that the vast majority didn't offer any training to line managers on budgeting. And of course most family-owned businesses would have even fewer resources to use for training. The good news is that, with simple training, the entire budgeting process for one manager would only take a few hours. And important functions like running reports to compare last year's budget with current numbers, or using a budgeting program would only take a couple of hours.

When offering training, it's best to start with executives who are willing. Some will appreciate that good training can convert an unpleasant task that they put off into a routine one. If your internal finance people can't do this training for your willing managers, your accountant or other consultant can handle it.

MAKE IT WORTHWHILE

The major reasons why managers don't like the budgeting process is that it takes time from their main jobs and they see no benefit from it. Finance ends up being a "policeman" trying to push budgeting on resistant managers. You need to set up a system based on communication to help line managers and finance managers get their jobs done. Involve them both in creating a new process that works for them and the company.

One way to change the budgeting process for the better is to eliminate it! An annual budget is quite arbitrary. It may be better to use a "rolling" budget for a 12-month period. That means that you update your planning regularly in little increments. And if circumstances change, your budgeting can change more quickly — like the reality of your business. For instance, if a new opportunity comes up, you expect to go after it. Or, if you lose a major customer, your budget should change.

Another problem is when you link bonuses to making the budgeted numbers. This encourages conservative estimates, but even then, final results are often out of an individual manager's control. There are lots of ways to set up a better system that encourages cooperation and performance. The best way is to get input from all your affected managers and let them design a system. Part of a bonus might be determined by overall company performance — thus encouraging cooperation. Part of a bonus might come from profits per department — thus encouraging profitable business, not chasing gross numbers. And part might come from other criteria like cost savings and new product ideas.

CONCLUSION

Budgeting is a function that can be valuable for a company to benchmark where they are, allot capital efficiently, improve communication about goals, and plan. However, in most companies it is looked at more as a useless annoyance. Few companies are ready to dump the annual budget despite the fact that it is often largely ineffective. If you involve finance and line managers together in a flexible process, you can turn budgeting into the useful process it was intended to be.

QUESTIONS TO ASK YOURSELF

1. Do I pay sufficient attention to my budgeting process?

2. Do line managers use budgeting constructively, or do they resent the process?

3. Can I improve communication between finance and line managers?

4. Could budgeting be used to focus on new priorities?

QUESTIONS TO ASK YOUR ACCOUNTANT

1. How can you help us with our budgeting process?

2. Can you provide training for budgeting to my managers?

3. Do you have any software you recommend for budgeting?

4. Can you help improve communication between finance and my managers?

CHAPTER 9

Controller Services

You have steadily grown your business and added people to the company — production, service providers, sales, administrative, and maybe even hired bookkeepers to take on some of the routine accounting tasks. But now growth has hit a plateau. You find yourself spending more and more time helping the various areas of the company to keep up their output. So much so that now you are spending more time helping everyone else than taking initiatives to build the business.

You are now so caught up in the daily routines of everyone's roles that you cannot give your highest-value contribution to your company — providing strategic direction. You'd like to hire more people but believe all that will do is add more people asking for your help. Finally, your family and friends are forgetting what you look like because you're spending more time at work trying to keep all the plates spinning!

ADDING FINANCIAL HELP

This is the point in time where you can benefit from enlisting professional help to change your status quo. One useful possibility is a higher level financial person responsible for organizing, directing, and controlling the work of your accounting function. Someone who can gather and interpret financial data for your use or the use of outside "stakeholders" — bankers, taxing authorities, or investors — and someone who knows how to structure the numbers for your management decisions. This person will measure the performance of your operations against budget, goals, and other benchmarking data to assist you in making better decisions. This person is most commonly called a controller.

A controller's role can range from someone able to supervise the current accounting personnel and provide some direction, on up to someone just below a chief financial officer. They can be full or part time. How you decide to use a controller will be dictated by your current needs and the things you no longer want to deal with on a daily basis. Your accountant is best suited to assist you in identifying the tasks this person should fill by asking you some key questions. They may also be able to fill the role part-time if you are not ready for a full-time employee. Other business relationships such as your banker, attorney, or insurance professionals can also give you input.

Your controller's job description may include several of the following:

- Management of cash and debt
- Inventory management
- Capital expenditures planning
- Establishment of accounting systems, controls, and software selection
- Accountant, banker, and investor relationships and communications
- Monitor departmental performance
- Produce internal financial statements for better management decisions
- Provide analysis of profitability and revenues
- Proposal review for benefit plans, property and casualty insurance, and equipment
- Selection of other outside service providers
- Recruiting, training, and retention of personnel
- Supervise accounting personnel
- Setting of budgets, business plans, and technology solutions

The list above focuses on the items that really help your business grow. There are also further statutory items that you and your company are responsible for each day, week, month, or year. If these are not done on a timely basis, you might have someone more persevering hounding you or possibly trying to put you into jail! These are some of the items you must comply with:

- Payroll taxes
- Sales and use taxes
- Franchise tax reporting
- Property taxes
- Corporate taxes
- Funding requirements (i.e., grant reporting)
- Accounting principles and standards
- Listed company reporting (SEC)
- Safety reporting (OSHA)
- Employment reporting (EEOC)
- Specific reporting for your industry
- Any other statutory reporting requirements

Using the above items as a checklist, you can prepare a job description for this controller role that will free up your time to do the things that only you can do. Hopefully, this will also create energy for you where it had been sapped before and give you joy. The more you need from a controller, the more you'll pay. Give significant thought as to what would give you the most benefit. The more your controller performs in the organization, the more:

- You will be freed up to build the business faster
- Profitability should grow
- You will rely less on your accountant to perform services for your business

TALES OF TWO BUSINESSES

Do It Yourself, LLC started out small, but has grown steadily over the last couple of years. From the time the company began, Do It Yourself, LLC experienced double-digit growth year after year. However, over the last couple of years, the growth rate has steadily declined. As the owner, Jack has been spending almost ten hours a day at the office, sometimes six days a week, trying to help each department work more efficiently. Jack thinks that if his departments are more effective, that maybe his growth rate will begin increasing again. Consequently, Jack is now racing to put out "fire" after "fire," and doesn't have room in his schedule to be proactive and plan for the future.

In contrast, Jill is the owner of a small business called Plan Ahead, Inc. After a couple of years of handling all the financials for the company, Jill met with her accountant to discuss the future of Plan Ahead, Inc. They worked on a strategic plan, and Jill hired a part-time controller. Now Jill gets a weekly review of Plan Ahead, Inc.'s financial information, and can stay on top of her accounts receivable to better manage her cash flow. With a clearer picture of her financial obligations, Jill is able to allocate a little extra money to marketing, which will help her continue to grow Plan Ahead, Inc. at a steady rate of 10–14% each year.

CONCLUSION

The best managers know how to delegate tasks that they *could* do so that they can do more of the tasks that only they *can* do. By leveraging the skills of others, you can do more of your highest-value jobs. The controller position is one that may benefit many businesses as they grow. Your accountant may be able to handle these tasks on a part-time basis or help you hire a person with the appropriate skill set.

QUESTIONS TO ASK YOURSELF

1. What could I do with my extra time if I hired a controller?

2. What are the tasks I do now that could or should be done by someone with more accounting expertise?

3. What are the tasks that take a lot of my energy?

4. What impact does the work I really love to do add to the growth of my company?

5. What are the character and cultural traits I should be looking for in a controller?

6. How much control am I really willing to give up?

7. What would be my return on investment (ROI) in a controller position?

Questions To Ask Your Accountant

1. What systems do I need that I'm currently missing?

2. Are the systems I need more project-based (one time) or needed on a regular (recurring) basis?

3. What would you suggest the controller's job description look like?

4. What level of expertise do I need to handle the job description and elevate my company to the next level of growth?

5. What should I expect to pay a controller?

6. How can you help me find the right person?

7. Do you have a qualified person who might be able to help me either on a temporary or permanent basis?

8. Would you recommend I start with a temporary controller first?

9. What temporary staffing companies would you recommend I use to fill this position?

10. Will this person help me offset any filing penalties I've experienced in the past?

11. How much will this person offset the fees I'm currently paying you?

12. What ROI would you expect I receive by hiring a controller?

13. How would you suggest I effectively manage this person if I'm not exactly sure what they do on a daily basis?

CHAPTER 10

The Value of
Audited Financials

The primary reason for having an audit is to provide an increased level of assurance regarding the accuracy of your company's financial statements. Having your financial statements audited can be difficult, especially the first time. Audits can be a lot of work. However, they can help you in a number of ways.

WHAT IS AN AUDIT?

An audit is an examination by an independent accountant of your financial statements for the purpose of expressing an opinion regarding the accuracy of these statements. Who can perform such an audit will vary by country and uses.

A complete set of financial statements includes a balance sheet, an income statement, a statement of retained earnings, and a statement of cash flows. An audit includes examining evidence supporting the amounts and disclosures in the financial statements. An audit also includes assessing the accounting standards used and significant estimates made by management, as well as evaluating the overall financial statement presentation. The company's management is responsible for the content and preparation of the statements, even if done by your accountant.

Many audits are performed because third-party stakeholders such as financing companies, vendors, and governmental agencies require them. These requirements stem from laws issued by governmental agencies, prerequisites for businesses to enter into a relationship, and expectations of owners and investors. For instance, in the United States, all public companies are required by the Securities and Exchange Commission (SEC) to have an annual audit, as are all large contractors, insurance companies, and banks by their respective state governing agencies.

In the US, if a privately held company wishes to go public they must have three years of audits on record. For privately held companies, the audit must be conducted in accordance with generally accepted auditing standards, while audits for a publicly held company must be conducted in accordance with the standards of the PCAOB. These standards require that the auditor plan and perform the audit to obtain reasonable assurance as to whether the financial statements are free of material misstatement.

Outside of legal requirements, many vendors will not extend credit, nor will financing companies provide funding, without an audit being on record. Owners and investors require an audit to help ensure the integrity of management and employees of the firm. Finally, in the instance of a not-for-profit organization raising funds through grants and contributions, the organization's credibility in the eyes of its contributors is greatly increased by the existence of an audit.

BENEFITS OF YOUR AUDIT

The benefits of an audit extend beyond fulfilling the requirements placed upon your business by others. The knowledge that management and employees in the organization will have their actions reviewed by an independent auditor provides a deterrent from committing fraud or embezzlement and contributes to a culture of integrity within the business. There is the possibility that the auditor may uncover fraud, saving the company from substantial losses to employee embezzlement or other types of theft.

For companies with absentee owners, the audit provides additional assurance that management carries out their responsibilities as delegated by the absentee owners. With the audit conducted by an outside and independent accountant, the opinion in the conclusion of the audit is far more likely to be objective and unbiased due to the separation of the auditor from those whom he is auditing. Qualified independent auditors are experienced in their specific industries, bringing an extra level of expertise to the evaluation of the financial statements. Another benefit is the issuance of a management recommendation letter by the accountant that highlights deficiencies discovered during the audit. The improvements suggested may pay for the audit process.

So to whom is the auditor responsible? In the US, on the highest level, the United States Supreme Court ruled in 1984 that the independent auditor assumes a public responsibility transcending any employment relationship with the client. The independent public accountant performing this special function owes ultimate allegiance to the corporation's creditors and stockholders, as well as to the investing public. This public watchdog function demands complete fidelity to the public trust. In other countries, the auditor's responsibilities are not spelled out the same way.

Ultimately, the auditor must be held accountable to truth in the work, regardless of the employer. The level of honesty in the work is directly related to independence; the greater the influence the employer has on the auditor, the less objective the evaluation of the financial statements will be. For that reason, potential employers of an auditor have a vested interest in maintaining the auditor's independence and, in doing so, they ensure the long-term profitability of their firms.

THE GOOD AND THE BAD

Just how valuable an audit might be can be seen in the case of a medium-sized, privately held manufacturing firm. They had a yearly audit done routinely. Most years the audit showed nothing special and they almost ignored it. Recently, the auditor suggested changes in their procedures and inventory management that produced savings that paid for the audit immediately — plus ongoing savings into the future. And last year when the firm had a tax audit, it went very smoothly with a finding of no additional taxes.

On the other hand, there are many cases like that of a private plumbing supply company that didn't do audits to save the expense. When a longtime, trusted bookkeeper got sick and stayed out of work for three months, they found that she had embezzled more than $137,000 from the company over a three-year period. (And after the auditor explained how she'd done it, they understood why she never took vacations!)

CONCLUSION

Having regular audits done isn't the cheapest and easiest way to run a business. But when was the cheapest and easiest way ever the best? Audits will give you an objective, outside view of your business, make outside stakeholders feel more secure, and suggest ongoing improvements. They can also reduce fraud and help you deal with tax collection agencies. What's not to like?

QUESTIONS TO ASK YOURSELF

1. Does it make sense to talk to my accountant about the benefits of an audit?

2. Could there be embezzlement or other employee fraud in my business?

3. Is there any chance I would consider going public or selling the business within the next five years?

QUESTIONS TO ASK YOUR ACCOUNTANT

1. How difficult or intrusive would an audit be for me?

2. Should I use a different firm to assure independence of the audit?

3. What could I do to improve my business as you see it?

CHAPTER 11

Year-End Tax Planning

W e all know the saying about death and taxes being unavoidable in the long run. Because the thought of paying taxes is a negative for most people, business owners often avoid paying attention to tax-related issues. Unfortunately, this avoidance of thinking about paying taxes often carries over to avoiding tax *planning*. The notion that it's a good idea to *plan* to pay taxes is foreign to most business owners. But, while very few people *want* to pay taxes, good planning helps you pay *the minimum possible*. If you don't plan, you very likely will end up paying more.

Year-end tax planning is important because it affects your business and personal cash flow. Money that goes to taxes is money that cannot be invested in your business, in your family's future, or in your lifestyle. Year-end tax planning is also important because taxes are one of the few cost areas over which you can exert some degree of control through decisions you make and actions you take concerning the timing and recognition of revenues and expenses.

How To "Plan" Your Taxes

In spite of the title, year-end tax planning should not take place at the end of the year. Rather, it should begin several months earlier. The first step in the process is to take a picture of where the business is at the end of October (assuming your business operates on a calendar year-end basis). This picture is created by the balance sheet and income statement for the business as of October 31. Of course, to do this requires that you maintain up-to-date financial records throughout the year.

The second step is to project your anticipated revenues and expenses for the remainder of the year. What do you expect to generate in terms of sales, collections, receipts, and so forth? What do you expect to pay out for expenses like salaries, payroll, rent, utilities, insurance, and inventory? These can generally be closely estimated by your controller or your bookkeeper working with your accountant, but they should be reviewed by you personally to make sure that the projections are reasonable. In both steps, you should include your personal information and that of other family members whose tax liability is linked to the business.

Putting these two steps together gives you an approximate picture of the business for the entire year. Now your planning can begin. The first question to consider is: "If we do nothing, what will it cost us in terms of taxes to the business and the individuals?"

WAYS TO REDUCE TAXES

Assuming that you have a federal, or state or provincial tax liability, you can start to look for opportunities to reduce those numbers. For your business, there are several possibilities to consider:

1. Make planned capital expenditures for fixed assets (machinery, computers, etc.) prior to the end of the year to take advantage of allowable expense deductions.

2. Accelerate payment of certain operating expenses, including bonuses to owners and employees, so that they are incurred in the current year.

3. Consider establishing a retirement or profit-sharing program, if neither exists, to create deductions for the business and additional economic benefits for the business owner and employees.

4. Review your billing and invoicing procedures to ensure that sales are not incorrectly anticipated and booked prior to the end of the year.

5. Review your accounts receivable for possible write off of uncollectible accounts. Remember, only accounts actually written off qualify for a deduction.

6. Dispose of — and take a deduction for — worthless inventory prior to year end.

For individuals, there are additional possibilities:

1. Do you have significant capital gains or losses on investments? Can these be offset by sales of other investment assets?

2. Can charitable contributions be made in the form of appreciated stock to avoid gains?

3. Can state or provincial tax balances due be prepaid?

4. Are contributions to 401(k), registered retirement savings plans (RRSPs), or other retirement plans maximized?

5. Should you use your gift exemption to shift income within your family?

These decisions should always be made in the context of possible exposure to Alternative Minimum Tax issues.

With timely, sound tax planning, you can take effective steps to make sure that you pay no more than necessary while minimizing the impact of taxes on your business and your family. You will also be able to determine your impending tax obligation and be able to factor that into your cash management strategy for your business and personal circumstances.

Best of all, you will avoid surprises — something no business owner likes. Cost control is an essential ingredient to the success of any business. Proper planning helps reduce your tax costs.

Your accountant is your best resource for year-end tax planning because accountants understand the regulations and opportunities. Planning is an activity to take seriously yet most business owners do not have the time or the expertise to undertake it on their own. Those who try will likely find, at some point, that they have missed out on significant tax-savings opportunities.

Why Don't People Plan To Save Money?

There are many reasons why business owners neglect year-end tax planning. There are always important matters to attend to and fires to put out. In the category of being "penny wise and pound foolish," some business owners fail to do this in order to avoid accountants' fees. Others may suffer from the lack of accurate interim financial data about their businesses. They rely on their accountants to come in at year end to clean up their records and tell them how well the business did.

Not knowing your tax liability before the end of the year can have significant consequences for the business owner. You might use profits from the business to purchase inventory or other assets and then not have the cash to pay taxes. With proper planning, you can set a reserve aside to cover the known tax liability. Or you might miss an opportunity to accelerate purchases of fixed assets planned for next year into the current year thus reducing this year's tax bill.

The process of identifying projected profits and taking steps to reduce taxes can give you additional benefits. It can force you to make difficult decisions that might otherwise be put off. Writing off old accounts receivables or disposing of obsolete inventory can be unpleasant or even painful. Business owners don't like to admit their mistakes. But acting in a planned manner can make you money through tax savings.

A Tax-Planning Calendar

The sequence of events for business year-end tax planning with fiscal years ending on December 31 looks like this:

- **October 31 (or soon thereafter).** Produce financial statements for the business as of 10/31.
- **By November 15.** Meet with your accountant to project revenues and expenses for November and December. The accountant then develops preliminary tax projections.

- **First week of December**. Evaluate potential tax-saving opportunities and required actions as recommended by your accountant.
- **By December 15**. Implement your decisions while your accountant develops final tax projections based on the impact of the recommended actions.

CONCLUSION

It seems obvious that accountants would argue for tax planning. What accountant would tell you *not* to plan? We know that taxes are something most people like to avoid thinking about. That's one reason they have an accountant. There is value in planning ahead. Once you build in yearly tax planning, it will be relatively painless and profitable for you and your business.

QUESTIONS TO ASK YOURSELF

1. Where does my business stand in terms of profitability at the end of October?

2. What can I anticipate adding to the bottom line by year end?

3. If I do nothing, how much will I owe in taxes?

4. How will that tax liability affect the cash flow of my business?

5. Should I incorporate any estate planning as part of my year-end planning?

QUESTIONS TO ASK YOUR ACCOUNTANT

1. What *must* I do prior to year end?

2. What can I do after year end (for example, accruals)?

3. Will I or my business be subject to the alternative minimum tax?

4. If so, how do we plan around it?

5. What changes in the tax law have occurred that affect my business or personal situation?

6. How will the decisions made for the business impact my personal return and cash flow?

7. What strategies can I employ throughout the year to reduce my tax liability?

CHAPTER 12

Tax Return Preparation for the Family Business

As a family business owner, you have many hats to wear and are expected to be pretty good at most of them — you really have no choice in the matter if you build a successful business. One area in which others do not expect you to be the expert is your company's tax return preparation. As the owner, you have so many other productive tasks to spend your time on that this is not an area where it is cost effective to do yourself.

There are several ways today to get your business and personal returns completed. You could do it yourself with some high-quality tax software available at your local retailer. There are also a number of tax preparers who learned how to do their own and started to do others for part-time income. Of course there are the well-known, nationwide companies that have several locations in just about every city. Lastly, you can use your local accounting firm. Let's take a look at why your accountant is your best choice as a family-business owner.

You And Your Accountant

Your advisor should know the accounting-related aspects of your business almost as well as you do. If you have been working with them on other projects, they are aware of many details even you may overlook. They may ask you a question like "Didn't you buy that new press last year?" Tax codes change every year so you need to have someone who has kept up on all those changes and how they specifically impact your business. Your accountant also has continuing education requirements to stay current in both technical and ethical matters not required of other preparers who may do your business returns.

You don't want any mistakes with tax collection agencies. Mistakes increase your odds of being audited. Each year your accountant is also made aware of potential "high-risk" areas for your business through training and current literature surrounding the tax audit strategy (the factors that trigger audits). They will work with you on these problem areas in the year-end tax planning (see

Chapter 11) so that you will avoid those landmines. And, in the US, if you are ever called in for an IRS audit, your accountant is one of only three individuals who can represent you before the IRS.

Another reason why it is useful to have your accountant prepare your return is to have that ongoing contact with your business. Their involvement in this part of your business is critical to identifying other key factors for you to consider, like where the financial leaks are in your business. For example:

- Is it possible that you have inventory shrinkage that you're unaware of for the year?
- Have labor costs risen disproportionately when compared to other economic factors?
- Is your debt service out of line with others in your industry?

What about opportunities that you may be missing? The following may be other significant reasons to use your accountant:

- Do you have a large amount of cash sitting idle?
- Are there subcontractors that can manufacture portions of your product at a lower cost?
- Are there tax credits for your industry you may be missing?

By working with your accountant, you have a co-pilot for your business. They are a resource for knowing things about the tax side of your business when you don't have the time. You want your accountant for your family business to know your common industry issues and the items you need to be concerned with in your business. Your issues are different than the *Fortune* 500 companies, so don't hire someone who has only done accounts payable for most of their professional career with a large company.

How To Make Best Use Of Your Accountant

1. During the year, ask your accountant if there are some tools he or she has that would make your year-end tax

preparation easier. Maybe they've developed a spreadsheet to make your home-office deductions simpler and more accurate.

2. Your accountant probably has a tool called a Tax Organizer that you can use as a checklist to help gather all the information they will need to prepare your return. It may even be available electronically so that they won't have to enter the data you submit to them and it can flow seamlessly into their tax software.

3. Set your appointment early in the tax season. Many people procrastinate and put it off as long as they can but this makes it more likely that you won't get as much time in your face-to-face meeting to discuss your return.

4. Keep a list of questions you have for your accountant. This way you won't forget some questions and will reduce the number of follow-up calls.

Each one of these steps will reduce the amount of time your accountant will need to prepare your return. Since most bill by the hour, this should also help reduce the fees you'll pay.

THE VALUE OF EARLY TAX PLANNING

Frank Martin's company had its best year ever last year. As such, he was concerned about tax liability. After the first quarter numbers were finalized, he sat down with his advisor in May that year to plan out the rest of the year's tax estimates. They discussed the improvement in the company's results and realized the investment they put into two new lathes had cut waste in half and increased production by 24%. Frank's accountant suggested that they take a look at a research and development tax credit they might qualify for since the definition had recently been broadened (see more on R&D in Chapter13).

It turns out that Frank's company did qualify for the credit as a direct offset against their tax liability from the increased profitability. They met again in early November to make sure their numbers were still accurate. They determined that Frank and some other key personnel could get large bonuses this year as another way to offset some of the company's profits.

Frank had his staff pull together all the information they needed and sent it to their accountant in late January. When he met again with his accountant in mid-February, they again discussed their strategy for the current year that was already ahead of last-year's numbers. Their tax return was submitted March 15th with a check for a couple thousand dollars since December closed out stronger than they had expected.

PROBLEMS WITH LAST-MINUTE TAX RETURNS

Ed Cannady always dreaded the whole process of pulling his tax information together. He never got started until a few weeks before the filing deadline each year. This year was especially difficult since his previous accountant had passed away. He had been a dear family friend for over 30 years and had done the taxes since Ed's father started the company.

Ed contacted several accountants and found that of the two who actually took his call at that late date — their fees would have been four to five times more expensive than his previous accountant. Ed finally found one of the national tax-preparation firms to do his return on such short notice. He gave the box of materials to the preparer and was told to wait for their call when it was done. On the day of the filing deadline, Ed finally got the call. He rushed down to pick up the return and was elated that his company was receiving a refund of over $10,000. Never before had he received a refund that large. Then, a couple of months later, Ed got another call — to set an appointment for a tax audit. When he finally started looking through his return, he realized that significant revenues from another plant had been left out of his filed return. That's exactly how his return was chosen for a tax audit.

CONCLUSION

Of course accountants want to do your taxes — that's a given. However, good accountants should be trusted business advisors in general. They should be able to use their experience and knowledge of business to help you avoid problems and see opportunities. They should be a useful sounding board and confidante. Finding the right accountant for you will allow you to focus on the things you do best for both your family and your business.

QUESTIONS TO ASK YOURSELF

1. Did we have any significant additions, losses, or changes in valuation methods that we should share with our accountant?

2. Does my accountant seem to know my industry, needs, and critical issues?

3. How much time do I have to prepare my company's tax return?

4. Does my staff have the capabilities to do our tax return?

5. Has my accountant returned our phone calls answering our questions and concerns?

6. Does my accountant really listen and ask good questions?

7. Do we have the time and energy to go through a tax audit?

8. What impact would an audit have on my family and me?

9. Does my accountant answer my questions affirmatively or say, "that'll probably work?"

10. Have we prepared enough documentation for our accountant to do an accurate tax return?

11. Have I set aside time to visit with my accountant at a mutually convenient date?

12. Have I adequately prepared my questions and concerns for when we do spend time together?

QUESTIONS TO ASK YOUR ACCOUNTANT

1. How well do you know my industry and the small business environment?

2. Who will actually be working on my return?

3. How much experience do you have with my type of company?

4. How much will the fees be? Do you charge by the hour? by the form? a flat rate?

5. How much involvement will you have if we get audited?

6. Are you aggressive and like to explore gray areas with your clients or is everything by the book?

7. What training do you take during the year to stay current on tax law changes?

8. How big is your client base and will I see you on a regular basis?

9. What associations are you in that help you identify new ideas or services beneficial for my company and me?

10. How will you help me organize my company's information for tax return purposes?

11. Does your firm use a tax organizer? Is it electronic? Is there a way we can just download our annual information into your tax software?

12. Are there things we could be doing differently that would have a positive impact on our tax liabilities?

CHAPTER 13

The R&D Tax Credit — It's Not Just for High-Tech Companies

Typically, when people hear the phrase "research and development," they immediately think their company does not qualify for this tax credit. The United States Federal Credit for Increasing Research Activities and the Canadian Scientific Research and Experimental Development Tax Incentive Program, or SRED (both hereinafter referred to as "R&D credit" or "R&D credits") are tax incentives often overlooked by many qualifying companies. When compared to the traditional definition of R&D, the tax definition of "research and development" is quite broad in terms of the types of activities and costs that qualify for these powerful government-sponsored tax incentives.

BACKGROUND OF THE R&D CREDIT

The R&D credit is meant to encourage the growth and development of businesses. As such, it was intended for the credit to apply to a wider range of companies and activities in order to encourage corporate investment. The tax credit is also intended to make companies more competitive. The SRED program is Canada's largest single source of federal government support for industrial research and development. In addition to the federal incentive programs, several provinces within Canada and states in the US have their own complementary programs.

WHAT TYPES OF COMPANIES ARE GOOD CANDIDATES FOR THE R&D CREDIT?

As evidenced by the title of this chapter, the R&D credit is not only for high-tech, biotechnology, and software companies. Some of the best candidates for the R&D credit are found in the following industries: manufacturing, tool and die, agriculture, software development, structural engineering, food processing, and pharmaceutical, among others. If your company has invested time, labor, and funds toward the advancement of its products, processes, formulas, inventions, or techniques, then it may qualify for the R&D credit.

WHAT QUALIFIES AS "RESEARCH AND DEVELOPMENT" FOR TAX PURPOSES?

The definitions of R&D are slightly different in Canada than the US. But for all intents and purposes, the US Internal Revenue Service definition of qualified research as *activities performed to discover knowledge that is technological in nature for the development or improvement of a business component used for a permitted purpose in conducting a trade or business* fits well. This means that designing, developing, or improving a new product; developing or improving a manufacturing process or other business process; determining a formulation; programming a new software application; or developing an invention to be patented (regardless of whether it succeeds or fails), for your business are all potential qualifying projects or activities with regard to the R&D tax credit.

Specifically, to receive the R&D credit, the qualifying activities performed must meet four qualifications:

- The activity must be related to the development or improvement of a business component (product, process, formula, invention, software or technique).

- There must be some uncertainty as to the method, capability or design of the business component.

- There must be a process of experimentation to overcome the uncertainty.

- The activities must relate to one of the "hard sciences" (for example, engineering, chemistry, physics, biology, biotechnology, computer science, and so forth).

In Canada three very similar types of research categories are eligible for SR&ED benefits:

- Basic research — work performed for the advancement of knowledge and science without any practical application in mind.

- Applied research — work carried out for the advancement of science with a specific application in mind.

- Experimental development — work undertaken to achieve a technological advancement in order to create, or improve materials, products, or processes.

For SR&ED purposes, three criteria must be met:

- There must be some type of technological advancement sought by the project or activity undertaken.

- There must be some type of technological uncertainty at the outset of the project or activity.

- A systematic investigation must be utilized towards eliminating the technical uncertainty present.

The activities that can qualify for the R&D credit can be large-scale business developments or small-scale process improvements. The scope of the project is immaterial, as long as the activities relate to the advancement of the underlying business. The start-up of a new business or a new division often involves a significant number of qualifying activities. For example, in many cases, the entire business process must be developed, tested, evaluated, and modified until it is operating smoothly. You may qualify for the credit without realizing it. Simple examples that may qualify for the R&D credit include the testing of an alternative raw material for potential cost savings, or the alteration of a process in an effort to reduce lost product, increase throughput, and maximize overall efficiency.

Oftentimes, the normal day-to-day activities that company personnel conduct may qualify for the R&D credit. For example, the systematic trial-and-error process and associated testing and redesign work that is employed during the development or improvement of a product design is often taken for granted as just "getting the job done." While these activities may seem routine, they constitute a process of experimentation that is undertaken to "get the job done" and may, in fact, qualify for the R&D credit. Furthermore, success is not a requirement in order for a company to claim the R&D credit for a particular project or activity. The nature of the qualifying activities and the intent of the project to advance the underlying business are sufficient to claim the R&D credit.

What Types Of Costs Qualify For The R&D Credit?

The expenditures that may be applied toward the R&D credit include in-house research expenses as well as contract research expenses. The in-house research expenses that can qualify for the R&D credit fall into two categories: a) wages paid to company employees for conducting, directly supporting, and directly supervising qualified R&D activities, and b) the cost of supplies used or consumed in relation to these R&D activities. Additionally, some capital costs associated with the SRED credit may also be deductible for Canadian companies.

The time and effort devoted to conducting research does not necessarily have to be undertaken by your employees. Contract research expenses are those amounts paid to anyone outside the company performing qualifying research activities on your company's behalf. By contracting with outside individuals or companies to conduct these activities on your behalf, provided their contract expenses qualify for the R&D credit, you are improving and advancing your company and, as such, those expenditures may qualify for the R&D credit.

Benefits Of The R&D Credit

In general, in the US, claiming the R&D tax credit results in a net cash benefit of 6.5% of "qualified research expenditures." Thus, for every $100,000 of identified, qualified research expenditures, the company will typically receive $6,500 of R&D tax credit. However, this net benefit calculation is subject to certain limitations that you can discuss with your accountant or other expert. In Canada, companies that have qualifying research and development activities are entitled to either a 35% or 20% investment tax credit, depending on the type of company.

The R&D credits offer a greater financial return than simply deducting or capitalizing the costs of the research activities. The

R&D credit is a "dollar-for-dollar" reduction of a company's tax liability. Furthermore, if there are any excess credits available — that is, excess credits after any refund amounts are received — these credits can be carried forward for up to 20 years in the United States and ten years in Canada, providing financial benefits from today's activities for years to come.

Lastly, claiming the R&D credit potentially creates a vehicle by which to realize additional tax savings in the future. It can lower your company's overall effective tax rate as well as increase the market value and earning power of your company. The R&D tax credit provides a return on your investment in ideas and concepts that are new to your company, thereby encouraging future investments.

Companies that elect not to claim the R&D credit may be declining revenue that they have rightfully earned. Such companies may find themselves at a significant disadvantage in the competitive business world.

CONCLUSION

The United States and Canada offer some of the world's richest R&D tax incentives, but many companies are not taking advantage of them to get the cash they deserve. As the pace of business accelerates and competition increases, small to mid-size companies may be more likely to overlook this source of cash because many lack the time, resources, or expertise needed to identify and manage such research tax credit claims.

Both the United States and Canadian governments have intentionally broadened the definition of businesses that may benefit from the R&D credit in order to stimulate the economy and reward those companies that undertake activities to make their chosen field more efficient and innovative. Companies continually participate in these activities simply to remain competitive, without realizing that their daily operations may also entitle them to tens of thousands of dollars in tax incentives. If your company is in any one of the industries described earlier, you may be a candidate for this powerful government tax incentive.

QUESTIONS TO ASK YOURSELF

1. Do any of my company's activities meet the qualifications for the US or Canadian tax credit?

2. Does my company design, develop, or manufacture new or existing products?

3. Does my company attempt to improve its existing products or formulas, or find new ways to use or manufacture those products or formulas?

4. Does my company look for ways to improve its internal processes or techniques?

5. Does my company develop inventions or obtain patents?

6. Does my company develop or engineer software applications?

7. Is my company in one of the industries described earlier?

QUESTIONS TO ASK YOUR ACCOUNTANT

1. Am I eligible for the R&D credit?

2. For all open tax years, what is the amount of regular tax and tentative minimum tax I am paying?

3. Approximately how much would I save each year by applying for R&D credits?

4. What are the benefits if I'm in a net operating loss or alternative minimum tax position?

5. How would an R&D credit affect the state or provincial taxes I pay?

CHAPTER 14

Cost Segregation: "Extra" Depreciation for You

As a business owner, how can you legally save tens of thousands of dollars on your tax bill? If you own commercial real estate in the United States, it may be easier than you think. Depreciation on real estate is a tax deduction that does not relate directly to the actual value of your real estate. Depreciation is a great tax deduction because you save money now, despite the fact that your building is normally going *up* in value, not *down*.

If you depreciate your building down to zero, you still have a number of options to avoid or delay taxes. For instance, if you give the building to other family members, they get to value it at current market value for their estates. By giving part of the building each year to several children or grandchildren, for instance, the gifts might fall under your tax free $10,000 per year. You then pay rent to them on that portion of the building, which is tax deductible for your business. Other approaches include 1031 exchanges with a rental agreement, or exchanging and moving to a better facility.

COST SEGREGATION DEDUCTIONS

Cost segregation is the separation of your commercial real estate into its components (carpet, millwork, computer wiring, and so forth) with different depreciable life spans.

The cost of your commercial realty must generally be depreciated over 39 years using straight-line depreciation. However, a substantial portion of the cost of a building may actually be written off over a much shorter period. This results in enormous tax savings for a building owner. In fact, thanks to economic stimulus packages passed in recent years, a building owner may be able to take advantage of a 50% "bonus depreciation" on certain portions of his investment.

The key to taking advantage of these faster write-offs is a clear and objective definition of three broad categories of construction costs: building, land improvements, and tangible personal property. Unfortunately, the distinction between what constitutes "personal property" versus "building" is not always entirely clear. However, the definitions of those terms can be determined through a complex linkage to a considerable body of cases and rulings dating back to the Investment Tax Credit, which was repealed by the 1986 Tax Reform Act.

Until recent years, the IRS (and consequently taxpayers and their advisors) worked under the premise that all costs incurred in a construction contract or real estate purchase were real property costs and should be depreciated as such. In other words, the whole "building" was depreciated evenly over 39 years with straight-line depreciation.

"EXTRA" DEPRECIATION FOR YOU

In 1999, after losing many court cases, the IRS recognized that certain real estate costs could be classified as personal property, despite the fact that the costs were incurred as part of a construction contract or building purchase. Additionally, the IRS accepted cost segregation studies as a legitimate method to separate structural building costs from other costs that receive more favorable tax treatment. A cost segregation study can uncover those hidden tax savings by helping you maximize depreciation expenses, thus lowering your taxable income via a non-cash expense (extra depreciation).

What qualifies? Automobile dealerships, nursing homes, storage facilities, apartment buildings, medical centers, hotels, restaurants, office buildings, retail facilities, gas stations, convenience stores, fast food properties, and a host of others can all qualify. Items specifically deductible are millwork, telephone and computer wiring, special lighting, process piping, storage tanks, oxygen systems, kitchen equipment, special construction to accommodate equipment, and the usual occupancy items such as carpet and wall coverings. These items are identified by examining blueprints, cost records, contractor bid sheets, change orders, fixed asset ledgers, and other records.

Use A Formal Cost Segregation Study

As stated earlier, the IRS agreed in 1999 that different classes of property do exist within a building. However, the IRS indicated that a "cost segregation study" is necessary to define assets that constitute tangible personal property. The IRS defines a cost segregation study as an engineering or architectural report based on contemporaneous data, *not* taxpayer estimates with no supporting documentation. In other words, you cannot take advantage of accelerated depreciation without consulting the appropriate experts, such as construction engineers, real estate appraisers, or someone with the appropriate knowledge base to perform such a study.

Studies breaking down costs into different lengths of deductibility can be performed on new construction and buildings (and additions) which have been in place after 1987. New ownership of real estate will get the benefit of the study over the next 5, 7, or 15 years, depending on the type of property reclassified. Owners who acquired their facilities in prior years are allowed to deduct their depreciation differences (catch-up) in the year the study is made. An owner who acquired the real estate five years prior to the study will take a 100% write-off on the remaining book value of five-year property in the year the study is made. To the extent the deductions exceed taxable income, the loss can be carried back and applied against the previous two years taxes. Significant refunds have been generated by use of this option.

On December 16, 2004, the Internal Revenue Service issued its *Cost Segregation Audit Techniques Guide* for use by its agents. The guide says:

> ...there are no standards regarding the preparation of these (Cost Segregation) studies. Accordingly, studies vary widely in methodology, documentation, depth, format and expertise. This lack of consistency, coupled with the complexity of the law in this area, often results in an examination that is controversial and burdensome for all parties.

While not required, it is highly recommended, that the preparers of your cost study use an engineering approach which includes a physical inspection of the facility, a study of plans and blueprints, and a systematic method of identifying components and costs. The study should be documented detailing project costs, cost summaries by appropriate IRS class lives, property definitions, study procedures, photographs, and the final results of facts to be used for income tax purposes. It is helpful to have items that are re-characterized supported by specific case law or IRS rulings or procedures where available. Some owners of real estate have used their own accountants, contractors, engineers, and architects to identify candidates for reclassification. While not required, the use of a firm that specializes in this area may provide a study that is substantiated and documented in such a way as to be more likely accepted under examination. Experienced preparers of cost segregation studies usually have compiled a list of components that are subject to reclassification and those which have previously been subject to clarification under audit.

BENEFITS TO YOU

In practical terms, what does this mean to you, the business owner? As much as 40% of the cost of a building, and sometimes more, may be classified as tangible personal property and depreciated over 5 years (or land improvements, depreciated over 15 years).

If you already own a building that was placed in service in a previous year, you can still reap the benefits of properly reclassifying the cost of the building. A series of Revenue Rulings from the IRS beginning in 1996, have established the procedures for making a "Change in Accounting Method" to implement such a change. Essentially, you can recalculate the depreciation you should have taken in previous years and take any excess depreciation as an adjustment on your most current tax return. In other words, it is not necessary to amend prior tax returns.

EXAMPLES OF THE FINANCIAL IMPACT

To illustrate the tax effect of this, let's assume Business Owner A constructed a building in 2004 and is able to classify $500,000 of the total cost as tangible personal property, eligible for the 50% bonus depreciation prescribed by the Jobs and Growth Tax Relief Act of 2003. Under this scenario, the taxpayer will have saved over $100,000 in federal income taxes in 2004! Over the first four years he owns the building, the tax savings are over $150,000.

Now consider Business Owner B who built a very similar structure across town. However, Business Owner B did not have a cost segregation study performed on his property. As a result, he will now overpay more than $100,000 in federal income taxes in 2004 because the property was not properly categorized on his depreciation schedule.

Of course, these taxes are only deferred until later years. The true value of a cost segregation study is best illustrated by considering the present value of the early years' tax savings, less the later years' tax deficits, discounted to current-year dollars. In the example presented above, the present value of Business Owner A's tax deferrals over the 39-year life of the property, assuming a discount rate of 8%, is still over $80,000. Generally, for every $1 million of 39-year property reclassified as five year property, the present value of your cash flow will be about $200,000.

To find out if cost segregation will work for you, you should first consult your tax advisor to make sure that you are maximizing this under-utilized strategy. One very easy way to determine that your assets are being properly depreciated is to take a quick glance at your depreciation schedule. There should be anywhere from 5–10 separately listed assets that comprise your investment in the building, with several of the assets being depreciated over shorter periods than the standard 39 years. If there is a single line-item with the description "building" being depreciated over 39 years, you might be looking at an opportunity to recast your depreciation schedule.

CONCLUSION

Depreciation on real estate has always been an excellent tax break. Any taxpayer with a substantial investment in commercial realty may be able to greatly reduce his tax bill by having a cost segregation study performed on his buildings. Cost segregation studies may provide you with a tremendous opportunity to reduce your income tax liability and increase cash flow in the near term. The value of a cost segregation study to real estate owners can be substantial. By analyzing each major component of your facility you can enjoy a large tax break. It makes good common sense that some components of your facilities should have a shorter depreciation life. Your accountant should be able to help you determine how to reduce your taxes and claim your refund.

QUESTIONS TO ASK YOURSELF

1. Does my building include a variety of elements, some of which could be depreciated faster?

2. Am I currently claiming depreciation deductions on real estate?

QUESTIONS TO ASK YOUR ACCOUNTANT

1. Have you dealt with accelerated depreciation on parts of a building before?

2. Am I taking full advantage of the available depreciation deductions?

3. What parts of my building might be depreciable at a faster rate?

4. How hard would it be to claim the past accelerated depreciation I missed now?

5. Can you perform a cost segregation study, or can you recommend someone who can?

CHAPTER 15

Intellectual Property

Every business starts with an idea — something that makes it unique or special in the minds of its customers. And, every business owner has confidence that their idea is either better than the competition or that they can do it better. That idea or process is the foundation for the intellectual property value of your business. The more unique, the more potential value an idea might have.

Intellectual property can be found in many places throughout your organization:

- The name or brand of a successful business
- The unique formulas, recipes, and designs created by you and your employees
- Processes or procedures that generate efficiencies or lead to the creation of new products or services
- Contributions to the industry or field within which your business operates
- Articles and presentations you and your employees have generated to promote or explain your unique products or services
- Each and every one of the designs, sketches, and renderings you have generated in the development of any successful idea that documents or validates your claim to a process or product

ALL BUSINESSES HAVE SOMETHING

When we think about a business as simple as a coffee shop, our thoughts immediately turn to Starbucks. The idea of a stand-alone coffee shop is not unique in and of itself. They have been popular throughout Europe for years. When you look at the business model for this type of coffee shop, you begin to see that Starbucks was the first to offer their unique business proposition to consumers. This business has turned the simple cup of coffee into a social institution, and one of the more successful brands in the world of coffee since Maxwell House.

Not all businesses create a "brand" or even a unique product. There are many manufacturing enterprises that exist to create or fabricate parts or assemble products for other businesses without ever "inventing" anything physical. Think about Henry Ford's biggest contribution to industry in America — the assembly line. His process for doing business was pure and simple genius. His goal was to make the automobile affordable and accessible for the general population. With this simple goal in mind, he contributed greatly to the industrial revolution. Ford brought new meaning to the terms efficient and effective.

One final area within the world of intellectual property is the idea or creation itself. In its purest form one-of-a-kind artwork, original research, or a good book are the basis for this type of intellectual property. The real value or beauty of this type of intellectual property is in the eye of the beholder. A work of art in the simplest analysis may consist of a canvas, $50 worth of oil paint, and the talent of the artist. It doesn't have real value until a consumer or investor sees what the artist saw, or perhaps, something more in the creation itself. The same holds true throughout the creative world.

VALUING INTELLECTUAL PROPERTY

Placing a value on an idea is one of the more difficult jobs in valuing a business. One definition holds that the value of an idea is equal to the sum of all royalties that would be collected on an equivalent valid patent or copyright based on this idea. This assumes, of course, that the idea or product from that idea — a book, product, mathematical formula, or any other application — can be demonstrated in some meaningful way for the "consumer" to use.

Business valuation experts and other professional service providers can support the business owner to establish a value for the business, inclusive of its unique ideas, processes, and applications.

Other experts can also help to document the processes and ideas in such a way as to protect them from infringement. Copyright, trademark, and patent protections are three such tools at your disposal in the collection and archiving of your businesses intellectual property.

DOCUMENTING YOUR INTELLECTUAL PROPERTY

Dr. Stephen Covey, in his book *The Seven Habits of Highly Effective People,* suggests that successful people "begin with the end in mind." If the reason for your business is to be the best at what you do, then everything you do must contribute to that end. If you are going to become the most successful chain of coffee shops in the world, then everything you do must contribute to that end. Professional service firms should emphasize their differentiators so that the users see value in the services provided. This includes the area of customer service as part of the process of offering professional services. If you are a manufacturer, your processes and continuous improvement efforts must be documented in such a way that someone buying the business will be able to replicate your success. You must seek to keep your unique selling proposition (USP) fresh and you must protect your ideas and processes in every way possible to ensure that they have lasting value throughout the lifetime of your business.

It is essential that you "claim" your intellectual property and that you properly document your claim. Once you establish that there is value in the various writings, processes, and marks your business has generated, you must file the necessary paperwork and documents to establish your right to compensation for your creative contribution. I can only imagine the number of claims filed by Starbucks, NASA, or any single university in America since their inception. It is said that Thomas Edison filed more than 1,093 patent applications. Not every one was a "light bulb" but many contributed something toward another invention, many of which are still claimed by General Electric, the successor company to Edison's own "small" business.

At the very least, you must seek protection for your business name, logo, URL, and the "big idea" you will use as the basis for your business. Simple registration forms exist for these, and as you generate new ideas or publish articles you need to be diligent in your efforts to seek protection. Just imagine the lifetime value of the 1,093 patents created and filed by Thomas Edison.

Non-Registered Ideas

Not every idea and process is protectable with official filings for patents, trademarks, and copyrights. Some will be held as trade secrets. As your business grows and new ideas are created by you and your employees, you must have a way to capture those best practices, process improvements, and new ideas. There must be clear understandings between the business and the employees as to which of these the business owns, and to what extent employees participate in the rewards generated by any new idea, product, or process. Your professional service team can help you to generate the necessary forms and releases to ensure that your business really does own the intellectual property free and clear of any future claims.

Once you have some mechanism in place to capture these innovations, keep a watchful eye open to make certain that your system actually captures the idea. All too often we become so absorbed in the day-to-day management of the business that we forget to keep an eye *on* the business to ensure its future value to investors, heirs, or potential buyers.

In our experience, small businesses tend to fall on either end of the intellectual property value equation — from totally ignoring the intellectual property value proposition to capturing everything in the hopes that value can be established at some point in the future.

Recognizing Your Value

A business that specialized successfully in the printing of short-run cookbooks for the fundraising market developed unique expertise.

They actually helped the book industry innovate in this area by using existing technology in unique ways to "package" their printing process for clients across the country. On the surface, there was nothing so unique about their printing or binding processes that would make them stand out in this field. Essentially, book production was book production. What made them stand out and add value to this otherwise simple process was their unique approach to the marketing on a national scale of these otherwise local projects. They made these books "collectable" by pulling them all under one national marketing program. They literally created a market for otherwise unrelated products. Their unique business proposition had little to do with their "base business" and more to do with their customers' need to market books in a unique way. The trademarks and processes became a major part of the value of the company and were one of the largest assets in the sale of that company three years later.

On the other hand, there are businesses around the world that have yet to recognize the value of their own genius. For example, a colleague recently worked with a consulting firm in the professional services area to help establish a strategic plan for the next five years. They went through the usual planning process, but when it came to understanding their unique selling proposition, or their "value" to the industry they served, something became immediately apparent. As part of their normal business operations, they generated approximately 30 articles and presentations a year about best practices and innovations in their client's area of expertise. In this instance, they worked with the healthcare industry. They had hours of audio and video interviews, national speeches, and international presentations. In all, they had an archive listing more than 15 pages of intellectual properties of various lengths and formats.

One simple review made it obvious to even the casual observer that there was a gold mine of information waiting to be exploited. There were at least six major industry innovations identified and more than 50 best-practice captures that would help any one of their clients become leaders in their market. And nothing more than archiving this collection had been done. Perhaps the value of the work was viewed as the face value of the payments received for producing the articles. The real value to the firm's clients, when presented in proposals and planning exercises would be worth millions of dollars in revenue. Had this firm realized the real value of the collection, they could have marketed themselves as unique innovators and not just another consulting firm specializing in the healthcare industry.

CONCLUSION

Intellectual property is often an overlooked area for businesses. Yet even businesses that don't directly invent things produce ideas, processes, or product packages that have central value in their businesses. By focusing on such intellectual property, you can often increase the value of your business, as well as the efficiency of internal operations. In addition to formal patents, trademarks, and copyrights, clearly document your business intellectual property and protect it. This will repay you in both value and peace of mind.

QUESTIONS TO ASK YOURSELF

1. What have I done to protect the name of my business?

2. What is special about the way I run my business or the processes we use to get things done in my business?

3. Is there one area where I consider myself a market or industry leader?

4. Have we invented anything in the course of running our business that does not exist anywhere else in our industry?

5. What articles or interviews have we participated in to celebrate a significant business landmark or innovation?

6. Have we won any awards or been recognized by our community or industry for any contributions above and beyond our basic business?

7. What "research" or "design" work have we done as part of our normal course of business?

8. Have I saved my notes and doodles from the creative sessions we've held to solve particular problems we faced as a business?

9. Do we have a policy in place concerning the creation of new products, processes, or ideas generated by employees pertaining to the work we do?

10. What patents, copyrights, and trademarks do we own, and where is that documentation?

QUESTIONS TO ASK YOUR ACCOUNTANT

1. What is a business valuation?

2. Why should I engage you to conduct a business valuation?

3. How do I establish the value of the copyrights, patents, and trademarks owned by my business?

4. How should I document the intellectual property we currently own?

5. How long does intellectual property protection last?

6. Where do I look inside my business for the "real innovations" we have developed?

7. How can I participate in the ongoing royalties of the inventions and innovations we created after the sale of my business?

8. When do I have to file for the various protections offered in order to ensure maximum protection?

9. What is the return on investment (ROI) calculation to use in determining which ideas and processes to protect, and which to just document as part of the proprietary operation of the business?

10. How do I determine the ideal point in time to sell my intellectual property as a stand-alone idea versus selling the company for its maximum value?

CHAPTER 16

Working with Banks

A business of any size will eventually want more from a bank than just a checking or savings account. Your business will normally use a commercial bank for services like a line of credit, merchant accounts, equipment financing, loans, and letters of credit. Many business owners often overlook the fact that a good banker can also be a free business consultant (more on that later).

PICKING A BANK (OR TWO)

You likely already have a bank. But is it the *right* bank for you? The first thing to look for is a bank that is commercial, or business oriented. Some banks are largely commercial in nature. This includes the huge "money center" banks as well as local "boutique" business banks. Often these banks don't even make home loans. In other banks, they'll have mainly retail branches with one business branch, but the retail offices won't always tell you that unless you ask. While it's convenient to make deposits in your local branch, you should get to know the officers in the commercial branch. Ask your bank what their focus is if you are in doubt about their orientation.

When choosing a bank, we like the "Goldilocks" approach to matching your business to a bank. You want one that's not too big, not too small, but just right. The right bank for you will depend on the size of your business. Huge banks really aren't motivated by transactions of less than several hundred thousand dollars. Your branch manager may give good service and may be interested in your local community, but any big decisions usually are handled by loan committees elsewhere. Small banks with capital under, say, $400 million may give great service but are limited in the size of the transactions they can handle. They may be fine if your business does a few million a year in revenue.

In shopping for a bank, you want to look for stability, both in ownership and staffing. You want to work with someone who has been there for five years or more. And you want your banker's boss to have been there for a while so you won't be caught in the middle of changing policies. If you're a medium to large business, you should look for a bank with total assets of about $400 million to $3 billion. These banks are small enough to care about your business and large enough to handle almost all banking needs. If you find someone to give you good service, your needs can be taken care of. However, if you're a small business, you may be better off with a smaller bank.

Look at the bank's loan-to-deposit ratio. In the old days, if 80% of a bank's deposits were in a loan portfolio, that was considered aggressive. These days, a 98% loan to deposit ratio would be good. Or even over 100%! A bank's investment portfolio must be conservative, so it generates low returns. Aggressive banks with high loan ratios will be very competitively priced for you. They want to make all the loans they can because that's where their profits come from. Aggressive "lending" banks pay the highest rates on deposits, too. You're looking for a Wal-Mart type deal — lower margins and higher volume. You can find this kind of information on any regulated bank at www.FDIC.gov.

I recommend that you build relationships — and do business — with two banks. That way if your personal banker moves on, or your first bank turns you down on a loan, you'll have someone to talk to who already knows you. And by having two banks, you keep a little competition for your account — and bankers will keep their pencils sharp when pricing services and products. Each bank will always try to sell you on having everything at one place, but that is more for them, not you.

THE BEST WAY TO FIND A BANK

When business owners are looking for a bank, or banks are looking for clients, they both would like to have a referral. Your accountant is an ideal referral source for you. Business banks want to have good relationships with the accounting firms in town. Not only do they make prestigious clients themselves, but when financials come in from an accountant, bankers know they will be correctly, professionally prepared.

When your accountant recommends a bank — and a specific banker — you go in with a strong referral. Bankers like companies that have regular professional service providers, like attorneys, consultants, and accountants. It means they are managing their businesses better and get the help they need. Hopefully, your accountant has screened you to fit that bank. The banker will want to take good care of you because your accountant has other clients with that bank. If they neglect you, others will hear about it! Ideally, the accounting firm also has their own business account with the bank.

WHEN YOU NEED SOMETHING FROM YOUR BANKER

Let's say you are shopping for a new line of credit, or you want a loan to buy a building or another business. Bankers see a lot of business plans. They know that anyone can have a slick-looking plan prepared. And if it's a new venture, they know the projections are guesses (and usually overestimates at that!). An experienced banker has a pretty good "gut feel" about whether you are a good risk. More objectively, what they want to see is "sophisticated" management. By that, I mean that your track record is key. You have proven that you (and your team) know how to market, run a business, and focus on a bottom line. And great managers have high integrity. Great managers adapt plans to make things work when problems arise. Great managers protect their margins. They don't sell at any price and lose profit margins. Great managers control administrative costs.

Your banker wants you to have a very profitable business and make a lot of money. This makes you a better customer. It helps the local economy, provides jobs, and increases goods and services available. However, your banker also wants to see that you can delay self-gratification so your business growth will continue and be stable. In other words, people who buy a new house, new cars, and so on when they first achieve success may not be investing enough back in the business to ensure future growth. The research reviewed in the book *The Millionaire Next Door* shows that self-made millionaires tend to *under*-spend their incomes. They are conservative. They live in the same house for years, drive an older car, and save a lot of money. They live comfortable lives, but they delay immediate gratification for long-term success.

Bankers, like venture capitalists, want to invest in sound people even more than sound businesses. Any business can be successful, but it takes "sophisticated" management to keep it that way. This means that they want to know about you. If your personal credit report is a mess, they worry that your business finances will be a mess too. They can loan money against your personal guarantee and strong assets, but they don't want to own your house!

Working With Your Banker

As in all aspects of business and life, having good relationships with your banker can only help you. That means making a point to keep in touch with specific individuals at your banks. Say hello when you take deposits in. Invite your bankers to your open house. Get to know their bosses. Show them your yearly financials. Build the relationships. You may not need anything for years, but when you do, the banker will know who you are and that you are a solid citizen.

To be an entrepreneur takes determination and drive. But bankers also like people who are a bit humble. They say how they've done, they are proud of good performances, but they look for ways to improve. Bankers like to hear what went wrong last year and how you are going to fix it. Admitting mistakes is a sign of strength and honesty, not weakness. In fact, from a banker's point of view, the best executives to work with have been what can be called fire-tested. They've been up against the wall and dealt with it. They know how to handle difficulties.

Bankers hate surprises! It's very important to keep good communication with your banker. When things go wrong, don't hide. When you are going to have a problem making a payment, tell your banker *ahead of time*. That way they know you are dealing with it. And, after all, they may have helpful advice. If you picked the right one, they have useful information about your type of business. (If you want more statistics about your business than you can find, ask them about the *RMA Annual Statement Studies* on businesses by SIC codes and size.)

Success Can Lead To Failure

One other tip is illustrated by two actual cases. The best banker for you is not a "yes man." You want someone who has good judgment and a base of experience to help you as a free consultant. This means they will not give you money for projects that don't look good.

Take the case of a business owner who went to the bank with a beautiful business plan, big dreams and passion, and even some investor support. She needed some additional financing from the bank to make it go. Her loan officer said that the business was a bad idea and outlined a number of reasons why. In her enthusiasm, she went down the street to a "nice" loan officer at another bank and got everything she wanted. Eighteen months later, she was out of business. She filed bankruptcy, and the bank took her house. Later she told the first banker that the tough advice was what she had needed. She just didn't realize it at the time. Entrepreneurs need passion, but sometimes they also need the counterbalance of an accountant, banker, or other consultant to help them deal with the hard numbers.

In a similar case, a business owner heard about a property that was being auctioned for taxes on the courthouse steps that afternoon. The property was near others he owned and looked like a great bargain. He rushed to his personal banker and obtained a $150,000 cashiers check required by the auction process. He won the auction, but the property turned out to have other liens against it and a number of other problems (like environmental issues). It took him years to clean up the title. Sometimes a too-cooperative banker isn't what you need, and actually can be quite expensive!

CONCLUSION

Choosing the right bank for your size of business can be very important and your accountant can be your best referral source to a good bank and banker. Bankers want to make loans to successful businesses — it's how they make their money. They also know that good businesses are run by sound people of high integrity. The right banker can be your best free consultant. Like accountants, bankers have experience with a wide variety of businesses. They've seen what works and what doesn't. If you find the right ones and level with them, they can help your business do even better.

QUESTIONS TO ASK YOURSELF

1. Do I have good communication with my banker?

2. Have I been honest with my banker?

3. Does my banker give me advice based on his or her experience with other businesses?

4. Do they give me useful advice, even if it's tough?

5. Do I have at least two business banking relationships?

QUESTIONS TO ASK YOUR ACCOUNTANT

1. How many banks do you maintain good relationships with?

2. What bank and specific banker would you recommend for my business?

3. Can you prepare the financial reports that my bank wants?

4. Would you recommend that I switch banks or open another account at a new bank?

5. At what points in my business should I look for new services from my bank?

6. Based on your experience with other clients, is my credit line priced right?

7. Should I pay a little higher rate to avoid "points" up front and prepayment penalties?

CHAPTER 17

Marketing Is More than You Think

M̶ost people who start businesses are more interested in their product or service than they are in support activities like accounting or marketing. In fact, accountants themselves tend to avoid marketing. Large and small enterprises spend vast amounts of money to promote themselves and advertise in every conceivable medium known to man. Is all the money spent on marketing worthwhile? Does a small family business really need to market itself?

To answer these questions the family business entrepreneur needs to look in the mirror and ask, "Do I want to be the best?" Marketing is for winners. Individuals and companies that have what it takes to create something that no one else can duplicate. Think McDonald's, Wal-Mart, or Ritz-Carlton.

REAL MARKETING

Most people think of marketing in only one dimension. Don't confuse marketing with how to spread the word about your company. That's only a part of it. Marketing is more about what your company is and who it serves. Marketing defines who you are, explains what you create that is different, and tells the story of why your unique brand experience can't be found anywhere else. It is your willingness to commit energy, discipline, and vision to creating a personal connection with a customer who will be so happy with her experience that she will tell others about it. Think Starbucks or FedEx.

You can get started by identifying who your customers should be if you are already in business. That's right; marketing begins by choosing your customers, at least by type. Are you looking for customers who value low prices, innovative products, or solutions to particular problems? You can't serve all of these customer groups equally well, so choose the segment that allows you to be at your best. If efficiencies and buying power are your strengths, then you can likely market your company as a best-price leader. Perhaps you're known for expertise and collaboration with customers. Positioning your business as a best-solution provider would make sense for you.

After you have chosen a customer segment to target, you can begin the process of creating business processes that support your market position. For instance, an innovation focus will require lots of research and development resources, a culture that encourages employees to try and fail often, and a commitment to constant new product development even at the expense of existing product lines.

Each customer segment that you serve requires a different set of processes to support it. And you will be expected to maintain or regularly improve your processes just to keep current customers satisfied. There are plenty of books detailing how to identify your target market and customer segments, so let's focus next on how customers buy.

How People Buy From You

We won't have time for an in-depth discussion but experts have determined there are two forces at work in our heads: the conscious mind and the unconscious mind. Your conscious mind uses logic to make buying decisions — like how much a product costs or the way a particular feature affects performance. Your unconscious mind operates from emotion and instinct, causing you to make a purchase based on how the product might make you feel.

Your marketing efforts need to connect with both of these minds — taking advantage of functional needs (the conscious) and connecting the experience of your product or service with a positive association (the unconscious). In fact, branding is often designed to build long-term, positive emotional associations with what you offer. The best way to do this is to simply observe how your customers use your product or service. Listen to what they are saying about your company and employ a healthy dose of common sense to compile your own list of what triggers a purchase decision. As a starting point, you might think of two things: In affluent societies many people buy *wants* rather than needs because their basic needs are taken care of. Related to this is that many customer feelings revolve around social factors like wanting to belong and status seeking rather than more "objective" needs. Of course, if you're selling commodity items based solely on price, customer behavior is different. But even then, your relationship with them can give you an edge over cheap imports.

Remember that customer perception is reality — whether or not that perception is based on fact. What you think about your products and services isn't important; it's what your customers think — or feel — that drives decision making. This doesn't mean you can't change their perceptions — as long as you remember it is *their* perceptions that count!

Your USP – The Basis Of Who You Are

Before you design a snappy logo or write a clever slogan, take time to create your company's Unique Selling Proposition (USP). Your USP is what gives you an advantage over the competition in a way that your prospects and customers can see. USP was defined by Rosser Reeves in a book called *Reality in Advertising*. He said that a winning USP:

- Makes a proposition to the consumer that if they buy from you they will get a specific benefit
- Includes a benefit that your competitors can't or don't offer
- Is a strong enough promise that it attracts customers

Examples of successful USPs include the Domino's Pizza emphasis on fast delivery, Wal-Mart's image of being cheapest, and Volvo's emphasis on being safest.

Coming up with your USP can be hard. While there are a variety of methods for doing this, here is one that has worked well for many business owners. Write a brief summary response to each of these questions.

- Who are you and what business are you in?
- What people do you serve, or want to serve?

- What are the special needs of those people?
- With whom are you competing?
- What makes you different from those competitors?
- What unique benefit does a customer derive from your product or service?

Use your answers to create a summary statement of how you wish customers to perceive you. This core message becomes the focus of your marketing efforts.

Armed with a concise USP and a clear idea of your target customer you can plan your company marketing strategy and budget. Use promotion to "tell" others about your business. Promotion includes strategies like brochures, press releases, sponsorships, seminars, imprinted items, and trade shows. Use advertising to sell your products and services. Advertising mediums include newspapers, magazines, radio, TV, and the Internet.

Small businesses will benefit most from a well-planned promotional strategy since the costs are lower and it is easier to execute. Advertising is a riskier marketing method because of the high costs involved. Space doesn't permit a detailed explanation of advertising but it will always require a larger budget, placement frequency, and careful tracking to quantify results.

Effective marketing creates the "WOW" factor for your company and brand. It builds repeat customers, sets you apart from the competition, and fuels future growth. In short, great marketing can be your recipe for success, instead of just another chore that is not central to your business.

MARKETING AS IT USUALLY IS

ClockWorks, Inc. is a third-generation family business battling big-box stores and specialty retailers for a mostly suburban consumer watch and clock trade. To remain competitive they have reduced prices, cut store hours, and hired part-time workers. Their advertising budget was doubled last year to pull more traffic into the store, but with little thought to ad placement and frequency the impact was minimal.

In recent years Tim and Jill, the siblings currently managing the business, have vacillated between creating a high-end market niche and continuing to stock a full line of products and price points. They have always thought of their company as able to serve anyone who comes through the door, so selecting a specific customer base is daunting. Upgrading the sales and repair skills of staff has also been a struggle as several other family members work in the company and none has outside employment experience.

A recent attempt to computerize product inventory was resisted by staff but eventually implemented. Process improvement hasn't been a topic of conversation since the new procedures for handling special order purchases implemented last year lasted less than three months.

An industry advisor, hired to analyze the store's customer base, found an aging population with substantial levels of disposable income. This prompted discussions about launching a concierge service to handle personal shopping for seniors, but the idea was shelved as too expensive to implement. Meanwhile profits are shrinking, customer loyalty wanes, and the clock is ticking regarding the future of another family business.

MARKETING AS IT CAN BE

It's All About Time, Inc. really is all about clocks and watches. Jeff who founded the family business a decade ago is a master clockmaker. At age 35 he decided to follow his dream to own a business. Jeff knew he couldn't compete on price with large retailers and discount chains, but saw an opportunity to leverage his knowledge and experience building clocks by promoting himself as a timepiece expert. He set out to position his company as *the place* to shop for timepiece parts and difficult repairs and service. Jeff knew that most watch and clock owners in his community wouldn't be a good fit for his business so he crafted a Unique Selling Proposition that read in part, "Our customers will be upper-class consumers with incomes of $500,000 plus who own expensive timepieces and value personalized service and attention to detail." He was determined to be the best in this market.

Early efforts to reach his niche customers included a UPS-delivered gift box sent to a carefully selected group of prospects living within 20 miles of the store. In addition to a four-color brochure explaining his unique repair expertise and selection of high-end timepieces, each box contained a small, tasteful desk clock laser engraved with his company logo and phone number. An invitation to attend one of several free seminars about antique timepieces rounded out the package. Jeff had already prepared his well-trained staff to handle seminar responses and to make follow-up calls.

The unusual marketing approach paid off and Jeff soon had a loyal customer base that often referred others to his store. Over the next few years, the store continued to host seminars and customer appreciation events. Jeff often spoke to community groups and civic clubs about the history of antique timepieces, and a recently launched website sells hard-to-find watch and clock parts to customers around the world. The company can now afford to advertise but still places ads only in quality magazines that are read by the store's target audience.

Ten years later, It's All About Time, Inc. is still growing and Jeff regularly reviews his marketing plan and adjusts product and service offerings to meet the changing needs of customers. Every interaction with his company is orchestrated to match the high-quality image that Jeff has created and his products and repair work always command premium prices. It appears that this family business will stand the test of time.

CONCLUSION

Unless you have no competition, marketing should be a central aspect of your business. Good marketing will help you deliver better service to the customers who will appreciate it most and be willing to pay for it. Marketing starts with a definition of your USP — what you are better at; what you stand for. At the same time, you should define the kinds of customers you want to work with. Then your promotion and marketing should communicate your unique selling proposition to the audience you want to reach.

QUESTIONS TO ASK YOURSELF

1. Have I taken time to choose my customers? Are they focused on best price, best product, or best solution?

2. Have I created internal business processes that can deliver the value my chosen customer group will expect?

3. Do I invest in employee training, both technical and management or leadership skills?

4. Does my company have a Unique Selling Proposition statement? What do we want to be famous for?

5. Do I have a written marketing plan that details how I will effectively reach my target customers?

6. Am I effectively using promotional opportunities to tell others about my business?

7. Do we track the effectiveness of our advertising efforts and know what mediums reach our target audience best?

8. Are we willing to say "no" to prospective customers that don't match our target market?

9. Do we know why our customers buy from us?

10. What are we doing to align customer perceptions about us with our Unique Selling Proposition statement?

QUESTIONS TO ASK YOUR ACCOUNTANT

1. How can your firm help me with marketing planning?

2. How much should my company be investing in promotion and advertising?

3. I would like to know more about how to improve the company's business processes. Any suggestions?

4. How would I go about establishing a customer advisory board to give me feedback about our promotion, advertising, and customer service efforts?

5. I'm concerned about profits. How can I improve my margins without negatively impacting sales?

6. Where can we get quality management and leadership skills training?

7. What promotional and advertising strategies have worked well for your firm? Can I apply any of them to my business?

8. If you were our customer, what would you want us to be doing that we're not?

9. What do you think is the main reason customers buy from us?

CHAPTER 18

Referrals Build Your Business

Ask any good business how they generate most of their new business and they will instantly and enthusiastically tell you they do it through referrals. Ask them to explain how they *create* referrals and you are very likely to get a blank stare.

Referrals are the lifeblood of any good business. There is simply no quicker and less expensive way to build your customer base and increase your income than to double or triple your referral rate. It doesn't matter what type of business you are in, referral business makes you more money than any other type of new business. Referrals cost little or nothing to get and they come with the healthy endorsement of a friend or business associate.

As accountants, we believe in referrals at least as much as other businesses. Our best new clients come from referrals from our existing clients and friends. Even more, as mentioned in the banking chapter, your accountant is in a position to give referrals to almost any type of business. Accountants and bankers are probably the best general sources of referrals around. Most accountants have thought about when they're willing to give referrals and when they're not. And, of course, we've thought about the value of referrals to us.

REFERRAL GOALS

Referrals are a far-too-important part of your marketing strategy to leave them to mere chance as most businesses do. They must instead be sought from every customer, every client, and every supplier that does business with you. Furthermore they must be sought from all your business and personal relationships, from your accountant to your dry cleaner!

We all tend to get caught up in the day-to-day work of our businesses. By keeping the goal of referrals in front of ourselves and our staffs regularly, we can all benefit.

THE PSYCHOLOGY OF REFERRALS

Giving referrals involves two contrary impulses. On the one hand, people like to give referrals because it allows them to help others at low cost to themselves. It makes them feel good about themselves and be a "hero" to others. On the other hand, people worry about giving referrals because if something goes wrong, they may get the blame. And, if things go right, the thanks they get is usually small. Because of this ambivalence, it's easy to get some people to give referrals and hard to get others to do so.

Clearly, your job is to encourage referrals and also make it *safe* to give referrals to your business. The first thing you can do to improve your referral system is to ask for them more regularly. The second thing you can do is to thank people who give you referrals more consistently and forcefully.

In order to get more referrals and make the most of the ones you receive, you need to also look at your customer service. If you don't treat new customers well, referrals will simply make more people unhappy with you — both the new customer and the referral source.

The third thing you can do is give referrals more regularly. The fourth thing you can do is to identify people who will consistently exchange referrals with you and discuss how best to do it with them. We think your accountant and banker should be high on your list of such referral-exchange prospects.

REFERRALS ARE ABOUT RELATIONSHIPS

Happy customers and people who know you in general will occasionally think of you when chances for referrals come up in their daily lives. But that's not much to rely on. You need to keep in touch enough that your contacts remember you *all* the time. You want to build better relationships with people so that they want to help you. However, that takes time.

Perhaps the easiest way to keep yourself in others' minds and begin to build relationships with many people at the same time is to send out a regular newsletter. Using the Internet, you can publish an online newsletter (zine) with little effort. After asking people if they'd like to receive your free newsletter, you can send a brief zine monthly or more often. Give them helpful information in a paragraph or two and your subscribers will remember you. Once in a while you can ask for their input on something, including referrals.

While a brief online newsletter allows you to keep in touch with lots of people, concurrently you should also choose a dozen or two people to build more direct relationships with. These are your best clients or referral sources, or people who could become them.

Each person has their preferences for how relationships should develop. Some like to go to lunch, some to ball games. Some like to play golf, and some are devoted to the Rotary. Some work for an industry group, some play softball. One mountain bike firm we know found their lawyer because he was mountain biking on the same trail as the owner.

Other ways to build relationships with people in different categories include:

With clients:

- Seminars for them
- Seminars where they speak about working with you
- Focus groups, surveys
- Client advisory boards
- Open houses

With competitors:

- Cross referrals
- Establish a networking group
- Joint seminars
- Align with national firms

With non-competitors who serve your market:

- Joint seminars
- Cross referrals
- Mutual self-marketing group
- Mutual client meetings
- Open houses
- Offer or take continuing education courses

With others:

- Trade groups
- Tips, leads groups
- Volunteer work
- Leisure groups

Referrals happen when people remember you and want to help you. You can greatly increase your pool of referral sources when you make it easy for others to have relationships with you.

How To Ask For Referrals

There are many ways to ask for referrals, depending on your specific offer, positioning, and your personality. Some people just come right out and say it, businessperson to businessperson like this:

> Joe, just as you probably do in your business, we find we get most of our new business from other satisfied customers. Who else do you know who uses our services or products regularly?

(Notice that we assumed the person knows people to refer by asking *who else* rather than *do you know*? This subtle difference creates very different results!)

Or you might ask Joe if his customers, rather than his peers, could benefit:

> Joe, I am sure you have some customers who need
> help with _____.

There are many other types of appeals you can use. You can make a *personal appeal*:

> George, it would really help me if you could suggest
> two or three other people I could talk to about what
> we offer.

(Notice we set an expectation by asking for two or three other people not just others.)

When people want to help you but have trouble thinking of names, give them some categories:

> Who owns the most successful business you know?
>
> Who else do you buy a lot from who is top notch?
>
> What about your suppliers?
>
> What clubs are you a member of? (And so on.)

You can offer *rewards*. In some businesses, it's appropriate to offer rewards for referrals:

> You may not know that for every referral you give us
> who buys, we give you each XYZ.

Notice we reward both people so the referrer doesn't feel he or she is taking advantage of a friend.

You can *make it easy* to give referrals:

> George, here are five calendars to give out to your
> friends. There is an offer on them for a discount
> they can use.

WHEN TO ASK FOR REFERRALS

When is the best time to ask for a referral? The short answer is anytime; ask early and ask often. Early in the relationship can be the best time. It's a good habit to get into when you talk with people. When you've just met someone, it's logical to ask what business they're in and how they get new business. You'll both eventually agree that referrals are the best source and this leads easily to a discussion of referral ideas.

The second best time to ask for a referral is as soon as you have developed a rapport with someone. He or she may not buy and you may never see them again. Never let people leave without asking for a referral. After a prospect has told you no is also a good time. Sometimes they will give you a referral to make up for not responding themselves.

The very best time to ask for a referral is right after you have completed a sale with a new customer. If they've just purchased from you, they are very open to helping you. Over 80% of all referrals happen within six to eight weeks of selling to a new customer. This is the time when excitement and anticipation are always at the highest level. After that period, people tend to fall into their regular routines. You want to get them into the habit of thinking of you and giving you referrals.

BUILDING YOUR REFERRAL MACHINE

With all your tools in hand, it's time to commit to the development of a referral habit that will pay untold dividends over the course of your business career. (Even if you're not in sales or marketing, the ability to generate business — to be a rainmaker — makes you more valuable in any position.)

The first thing you must do to build a referral machine is to make a serious commitment to gathering referrals and following up on them. You can often double or triple your referrals by simply asking for them. Not sometimes, not when you feel like it, not when you are having a good day, not if you feel the prospect likes you, but ask every single time in as many different ways as you can until you get what you need. They say it takes 28 days of constant repetition to develop a habit, so give it a go, starting today!

Whenever you get a referral, try to find the connection between the person referring and the referral. Ask how Joe knows Harry. Ask how long Sally has been friends with Chelsea. Ask what line of work the prospect is in. The more information you have about the referral, and the clearer you are about the referral's relationship with the referrer, the better your chances of a successful new contact.

REFERRERS CAN DO THE WORK TOO!

Interestingly, the better way to get referrals is also easiest on you. When your contact is uncertain of whether someone would want to hear from you, they can be hesitant to give you their name. Just tell your referral source that you understand they might be uncertain and suggest that they call the people and ask if they would like to hear from you. This way they prescreen the prospects and give you a plug before you ever talk with them. This is more like a natural referral where the people are almost pre-sold before they talk to you.

SHOW YOUR GRATITUDE

As mentioned earlier, once you have received a referral, whether it works out to your advantage or not, make sure that you thank people. At the very least, you should send him a thank-you note. If the amount of money involved in closing the sale is substantial, consider sending the person who gave you the referral a suitable gift for his assistance. A book on a subject that interests him, a bottle of her favorite wine, or a gift certificate to a restaurant will go a long way toward ensuring that this particular person will continue to refer good prospects to you.

THE LAW OF LARGE NUMBERS

The more people you know, the more referrals you get! Now that's a pretty simple concept, isn't it, but far too many people involved in business fail to take advantage of this simple fact! Join the club or association in your town that will bring you into contact with the largest number of prospective contacts! This might be your clients' trade groups, a service group, or a general Chamber of Commerce.

Okay, there are already ten people in your field involved in the Chamber who are more established than you are, so what do you do? Well, before you take the next step consider this: More than half of them never go to a meeting anyway. Of the half that go, they only go once a year or spend their time in aimless socializing rather than building relationships.

If you still feel there is too much competition in the local groups you have considered, try a jump to left field and change the game. Join a related organization rather than the most obvious. Join the Chamber of the next town over, or instead of the Realtors association join the builders association or the mortgage association.

Referrals are the lifeblood of most businesses, but you receive good words a whole lot more predictably and effectively when you develop and follow a referral system so that you don't miss most of the possible good referrals.

A great referral source is someone who wants to help you succeed. They think of you all the time. They give out your card with an endorsement. They refer people to your website. They introduce you at lunch, and so forth. They may do it because they like mentoring you, because you refer back to them, because they're your cousin, or for other reasons.

CONCLUSION

There is no quicker, no less expensive way to increase your business than to build a referral system rather than leave it to chance, as most people do. Your system must be structured and measured. Then your staff must be trained and rewarded for following it. No less important is the recognition and rewarding of those who are doing the referring.

QUESTIONS TO ASK YOURSELF

1. Have I defined what a good referral is for me?

2. Do I reward staff for meeting referral goals?

3. Do we keep meticulous records of each possible referral source in our CRM system (database)?

4. Do we produce a simple online newsletter or some other tool to build relationships with prospects and referral sources?

5. Who can I talk to about mutual referrals who want me to succeed?

QUESTIONS TO ASK YOUR ACCOUNTANT

1. Do you agree that referrals are the best way to get new business?

2. When do you give referrals to clients like me?

3. What tools can I give you to make it easier to give me referrals (for instance, business cards, a sheet of tips, brochures, an article I wrote, and so on)?

4. Can we set up a group of your clients to meet and talk about mutual referrals?

5. Would you like a written testimonial from me?

CHAPTER 19

It's a People Business: Employee Benefits

You may not think of your business as a "people" business. Your numbers may depend on manufacturing, technical expertise, or something else that doesn't emphasize human resources. However, in a family business (and any other) human dynamics within the business can make or break your success. Family businesses not only have to deal with employees, but an extra layer of family dynamics.

Strong human resource practices have the potential to increase your company's productivity and profitability. It's important that you build an employee-benefits strategy that motivates your employees and increases loyalty so that you can retain top performers. Yet, as the owner of a growing business, there are a lot of compliance issues to deal with. Reports, paperwork, data entry, and HR administration can consume your valuable time and become an enormous task that demands considerable resources. And time spent on administrative functions is time spent away from growing your business. So what's the best solution for a small-business owner?

In 1914, The Ford Motor Co. revolutionized the industrial world. Henry Ford, the company's chairman and the inventor of the Model T, announced that he was going to start paying Ford factory workers $5 a day. That was more than double the minimum wage for that industry! Ford also reduced the standard workday from nine hours to eight. Competitors scoffed and criticized, but Ford gained employee loyalty *and* more people who could afford his cars.

Today the most successful companies offer substantial benefits for their employees, such as healthcare, paid vacation, flexible hours, daycare, and the list goes on. Why? Because good companies begin with good employees. And, in family businesses, benefits are often worth more than the salary they replace. Happy employees provide better service to each other and to your customers—and produce more profits for your company.

As you decide which processes can be managed in-house and which can be administered through external sources, remember that outsourcing certain functions, like human resources, can go a long way in providing the flexibility you need to grow a successful company.

Outsourcing Human Resource Functions

Outsourcing your human resource functions can provide administrative relief from many employee-related responsibilities so you can concentrate on developing strategies and working on your business. According to Frank J. Casale, chairman and CEO of The Outsourcing Institute in Jericho, New York, outsourcing "is the great equalizer for small- to medium-sized firms. Growth-oriented entrepreneurs…can benefit tremendously. Not only do employees frequently gain access to better benefits, [but] the owner gains freedom to focus."

The paperwork of the human resource function is an increasing burden on the small business owner. With federal and state or provincial regulations, changes in tax codes, and increasing legal liability for employers, the complexity of this industry has multiplied in recent years. For instance, the US Internal Revenue Service estimates that one third of all employers are charged for payroll mistakes.

Human resources is the most outsourced of all business processing functions. Outsourced, external service providers can help your company by offering administration and management for many primary and supplemental services. While it comes with a cost, it can improve employee service and maximize resources across your organization. Outsourcing these functions not only allows you to concentrate on growing your core business, but also frees up administrative staff to pursue more value-added activities.

Locking In Employee Loyalty

You get more out of your business when you get more out of your people. As it becomes more and more difficult to compete with larger companies for the best and brightest, there are a lot of things that small business owners can do to help attract top talent. With the right HR plan in place, you will find that retaining your top performers does not necessarily involve a higher rate of pay. Positioning your company as one that values a work-life balance often carries more weight than a large salary. In fact, 57% of graduating business students around the world rate maintaining balance between work and personal life as their primary career goal and rate it the key to choosing their employer, according to a PriceWaterhouseCoopers report. However, you need to sell this benefit. Otherwise employees — and prospective employees — may take for granted that benefits and lifestyle support is equal across businesses.

PROTECTING YOURSELF

Discussing your options with your accountant can be helpful in determining which human resource strategies are best for your company. We can help you protect yourself. Ultimately, you as the employer are responsible for the deposit and payment of federal taxes, as well as the timely filing of quarterly and annual reports. While many outsourcers will deposit and pay taxes on a company's behalf, if they fail to remit and file tax reports in a timely and accurate manner, you will be assessed. Therefore, extreme diligence is warranted before implementing any outsourcing arrangement.

Be clear in setting expectations, defining objectives and priorities, as well as allowing room for some flexibility as your business grows and changes. Choose an employment expert who understands your needs and wants, as well as what works in your particular industry.

OUTSOURCING OPTIONS

There are several outsourcing options available; it's up to you to decide which is best for your business. A few models to consider are:

- *Third-Party Administrator* — primarily deals in retirement plans, such as 401(k)s and registered retirement savings plans (RRSPs).

- *Business Process Outsourcer* — allows an employer to pick and choose which critical functions to outsource, such as payroll processing and benefits administration, while still maintaining control over others, like compensation and training. In many cases, the economies allow a company to expand services with little or no increase in cost.

- *Professional Employer Organization* — assumes all human resources responsibilities and employer risks for its clients, including labor law compliance, payroll, benefits, and employment taxes.

HOW TWO BUSINESSES HANDLED HR FUNCTIONS

As a young company, the owner of Top Performers, Inc. saw great profit potential. But she knew that it was imperative she spend as much time working *on* her business as she did working *in* her business. So she met with her accountant and developed a business plan and strategy for growing her business. She outsourced many administrative functions and hired a part-time administrator to coordinate their handling of all payroll processing and benefits administration. This left the owner with the time to work one-on-one with each new sales associate she hired. It was very important to the owner that each employee was as excited about Top Performers, Inc. as she was, so she dedicated time to coaching her staff and remembered to reward them and recognize them for their accomplishments. Year after year, her business continued to flourish, along with her employees' loyalty to Top Performers, Inc.

Implication Inc. started out in much the same way. When they started in business, they had few employees and business was booming. Growth hit so fast that the owner spent most of his time managing client relationships and dealing with mundane, yet necessary, administrative functions. To keep up with business, Implication Inc. hired several sales associates to handle the influx of prospective buyers. With minimal training, they were thrown into the proverbial fire. The number of closed sales began to drop significantly, and so did the commissions that the sales associates depended on to live. These sales associates worked harder at first, trying to close those sales to bring in the big bucks, but soon got frustrated with the lack of support and training from their manager (the owner of Implication Inc.). Soon the company began to suffer from high turnover, which resulted in more inexperienced and unhappy sales associates. This problem not only resulted in higher employee costs for Implication Inc., but in lower sales and profits.

CONCLUSION

Human resources are an easy area to overlook, especially for a family-owned business. However, how you treat your people can make or break your business. While you *can* get away with giving less attention to family members in a family business, they actually need — and deserve — better treatment if you expect them to contribute to the business long term. Outsourcing many benefits and functions can relieve you of paperwork and liability. When done right it can also reward employees and family while creating loyalty and better performance.

QUESTIONS TO ASK YOURSELF

1. How much time am I spending on HR paperwork?

2. Do I have a system to handle HR functions with little effort?

3. Could the time I spend on HR functions be used more profitably in another aspect of my business?

4. Do I offer a better-than-average benefits package?

QUESTIONS TO ASK YOUR ACCOUNTANT

1. Have you worked with HR outsourcing companies?

2. Have you assisted other businesses like mine with outsourcing their HR functions?

3. What are the tax implications of outsourcing?

CHAPTER 20

Why Your Business Retirement Plan Is Important

As a business owner you have many decisions to make when it comes to retirement plans. The decision to offer one or not is your first major decision. There are many advantages to offering a retirement plan for you and for your employees. Current and potential employees often consider an employer's retirement plan as one of the most important aspects of accepting or continuing employment with an employer. As a result, a retirement plan can help you attract and retain the most qualified individuals.

A retirement plan has significant tax advantages to both you and employees. Contributions are deductible as a business expense. But perhaps the biggest benefit is that contributions from both you and your employees are not taxed until distributed, and the contributions and earnings are allowed to grow tax free. Of course, you can also use your business retirement plan as a significant means to secure your own retirement.

How To Set Up A Retirement Plan

Once you've made the decision that a retirement plan is appropriate for your business, there are multiple steps that need to be taken. The first step is to decide which type of plan is the best fit for your business. There are many options available with the most popular being Defined Contribution, Defined Benefit, Simplified Employee Pensions (SEPs), and SIMPLE IRA plans.

Your decision about which plan to use will be based on many factors including, but not limited to, the demographics of your employees (such as age), the amount you would like to contribute for yourself and employees, the flexibility needed for employer contributions, and the importance of the cost and administrative ease associated with the plan. The decision of which plan to select should involve your accountant and any other advisors such as a third-party administrator (TPA) or investment advisor.

Having decided which type of plan is appropriate for your business, the second step involves establishing and implementing the plan. With the assistance of a financial advisor experienced in servicing retirement plans you should perform due diligence on the different providers available for the type of plan you have selected. This should include but not be limited to analyzing the menu of investment options, comparing fees associated with the different platforms, and understanding the different levels of services available to plan sponsors and participants.

Depending on the complexity of the plan selected, you may want to employ the services of a TPA. Generally, SIMPLEs and SEPs do not require the assistance of a TPA, while Defined Benefit and Defined Contribution plans generally need their services. All retirement plans are required to be in writing to lay out the specifications of how the plan works. Your TPA can assist you in adopting a written plan. Once the plan is established, eligible employees are notified and the financial advisor takes them through the enrollment process. As a family business, there are also considerations about your plan's treatment of family versus non-family employees. Under some plans, family members can receive far more benefits than other employees. At this point you have taken the steps necessary to provide a secure retirement for yourself and your employees.

OPERATING YOUR PLAN

After establishing and implementing your retirement plan, the next step involves operating the plan. Certain types of plans can be extremely complex. When it comes to operating such plans, the services of a third-party administrator will be important to the continued success of the plan. Your TPA will be responsible for the annual administration of your plan, which includes such functions as calculating the employer contribution, performing compliance testing, and multiple other responsibilities associated with keeping your plan in compliance with retirement plan regulations.

Generally there are several tasks the employer is responsible for, including ensuring eligible employees are covered under the plan, depositing contributions promptly, and distributing participant benefits. Along with the financial advisor, you are also responsible for managing the assets of the plan and ensuring that you are offering your participants the best available options. Finally, some plans require IRS filings, which are generally prepared by either your TPA or accountant. A strong relationship between all parties involved in maintaining your plan is essential for the long-term success of the plan.

By following the steps described, a retirement plan can be in existence for an extended period of time. It is possible that circumstances could arise requiring the termination of your existing retirement plan. When terminating a plan, your administrator will assist you in preparing the necessary amendments to terminate your written document. They will also provide notifications to participants explaining the effects of the termination. All participant accounts will need to be distributed and, if required by law, the final filing will need to be prepared by your TPA or accountant.

A GROWTH STORY

In 2002, we had a client who was poised for growth. They wanted to take the company to the next level and, in order to do that, they needed to have the right "infrastructure." By that we mean they needed the correct accounting, management, operational, and marketing systems in place. However, infrastructure is not enough in and of itself. They quickly realized that the key to implementing the correct systems was having the right personnel. They needed to retain their best people and in addition attract even more qualified employees. To do this they needed to go out in the market to compete for the best and brightest.

A key component of their strategy to attract the employees they needed was to offer a very generous 401(k) Profit Sharing Plan. Acting as the client's accountant and third-party administrator, we were able to assist in the design and implementation of the appropriate retirement plan. This set them apart from the other employers in the same market and led to some key hirings. This in turn allowed them to implement the required systems designed to take them to the next level of business performance.

All involved in this process believe that if the client had not implemented the retirement plan they would not have been able to attract and retain the desired employees. This would have had a detrimental impact on their growth strategy. In this particular situation the old adage, "you have to spend money to make money" was very true.

CONCLUSION

If you have employees, a retirement plan can be important in retaining them. If you plan to grow or give others more responsibility for management, a plan is even more valuable. You and other family employees can also benefit personally from a retirement plan and receive tax deductions. While there are many plan options, an expert will be able to help you determine the best plan for you.

QUESTIONS TO ASK YOURSELF

1. How important is securing your own retirement?

2. How important is helping your employees to secure their retirements?

3. How important is attracting and retaining qualified employees?

4. How important are fees associated with a retirement plan?

5. How important is the tax deduction?

6. How much flexibility is needed for your employer contribution (for example, are your earnings consistent)?

QUESTIONS TO ASK YOUR ACCOUNTANT

1. What are some of the tax benefits to me as an owner?

2. What are some of the tax benefits to my employees?

3. Given the demographics of my workforce what type of retirement plan should I install?

4. Explain to me the difference between an IRA, SIMPLE IRA, SEP Plan, and 401(k).

5. My profits vary each year — is there a plan that allows me to determine how much and when I contribute?

6. What plan would be best if I want to maximize the contribution for myself?

7. Should I administer the plan myself or outsource it?

CHAPTER 21

Analyzing the Value of
Your Business

When you make an investment, you want it to increase in value. If you own and manage your own business, you have made a large investment of time and money. In addition to drawing a generous salary, you also want its value to increase year after year. However, most owners spend so much time working *in* their businesses that they don't spend enough time working *on* their businesses to increase value. They may also lack knowledge of what it takes to create value. Knowing what factors impact value in your business and focusing management efforts on these is the key to value creation.

UNDERSTANDING VALUE

Common sense tells you that value goes up when your income goes up, your margins go up, and so on. To put it in more formal and mathematical terms, value can be defined by the following formula:

$$\text{Value} = \frac{\text{Income}}{\text{Risk} - \text{Growth}}$$

This can be expanded upon as follows:

$$\text{Value} = \frac{\text{Free Cash Flow}}{\text{Cost of Capital} - \text{Growth in Free Cash Flow}}$$

Free cash flow for the year is the cash available to the stakeholders after taxes, capital expenditures, repayment of debt and working capital needs.

Cost of capital is the weighted average of a company's cost of equity and cost of debt. For public companies, the cost of equity is reflected in its stock price, while the cost of debt is the interest rate required by its lenders. For private companies, where no market for the stock exists, the cost of equity is difficult to ascertain without the assistance of a valuation analyst. Like the public company, the cost of debt is the required interest rate of the lender.

Growth in free cash flow represents the estimated long-term annual growth rate of the free cash flow.

For example, given the following factors the value of the entity is $6,250 calculated as follows:

$$\text{Value} \quad = \quad \frac{\$1,000}{20\% - 4\%} \quad = \quad \$6,250$$

Free cash flow = $1,000
Estimated cost of capital = 20%
Estimated long-term free cash flow growth rate = 4%

In more practical terms, the formula above shows us that there are only three ways to increase value:

- Increase free cash flow available to the stakeholders.
- Lower the cost of capital by lowering company risk.
- Increase the growth rate of free cash flow available to the stakeholders.

DETERMINING WHETHER THE VALUE OF YOUR COMPANY IS GOING UP OR DOWN AND DRIVING YOUR COMPANY'S VALUE[*]

Managing the factors that affect your company's free cash flow and return on equity (ROE) will ensure that your overall decisions are increasing your company's value. ROE is important because it monitors the company's:

- Profit on sales
- Effectiveness in the use of its assets (asset turnover)
- Use of leverage or extent of debt financing

---

[*]*Driving Your Company's Value, Strategic Benchmarking for Value*, Michael J. Mard, Robert R. Dunne, Edi Osborne and James S. Rigby, Jr.

Increasing your return on equity normally indicates your company's risk and cost of capital are dropping which drives value higher. ROE is computed as follows:

$$\text{ROE} = \frac{\text{Net income}}{\text{Shareholders' equity}}$$

The DuPont formula breaks ROE down into the following components:

$$\text{ROE} = \text{Profitability} \times \text{Turnover} \times \text{Leverage}$$

Further expansion of the ratio results in the following:

$$\text{ROE} = \frac{\text{Net income}}{\text{Sales}} \times \frac{\text{Sales}}{\text{Total assets}} \times \frac{\text{Total assets}}{\text{Equity}}$$

By applying simple algebra, everything cancels and you are back to the basic formula.

MANAGEMENT FOCUSED ON VALUE CREATION

Now that you understand what makes your company more valuable, (more cash flow, lower cost of capital, increased growth rate) consider the following improvements by way of example.

- Recognizing the value of your customer base, you identify your top three customer-related critical success factors and establish key performance indicators to monitor them.
- Recognizing that faster asset turnover increases value, you focus on your credit policy and collection efforts to speed up accounts receivable collection.
- Understanding that faster inventory turns improve value, you eliminate slow-moving product lines and change purchasing practices.
- After performing a feasibility study for the addition of a major piece of equipment, you employ debt to make the

purchase knowing that the benefits from increased productivity more than offset the cost of the debt.

- It can seem counterintuitive to a conservative business owner, but by utilizing a reasonable level of working capital debt, you lower cost of capital, increase your return on equity, and level out year-to-year distributions to the stakeholders.

YOUR MANAGEMENT STYLE MAY HINDER YOUR BUSINESS

In our experience, the primary owners of family owned-businesses typically have either a sales, engineering, or financial/accounting background. Your management style — or combination of styles — influences the way you manage your business. Each style has its strengths for a business, but each also has its weaknesses. Too much emphasis on one area and neglecting another can hamper the growth of your business. Here are descriptions of these various management styles:

The salesman mentality. For this approach building relationships, keeping the customer happy, and making the sale are of utmost importance. These priorities can result in inefficient inventory levels, slow accounts receivable, and higher-than-necessary expenses.

The engineering mentality. Engineers are very technical, practical, and process oriented. Their businesses are most likely characterized by highly efficient operations and strong quality control. Because of their structural mindset they may struggle with the sales and more abstract financial sides of the business.

The accountant mentality. This one is probably the worst. (I can say that since I'm an accountant!) We understand what impacts the bottom line. We know that increasing inventory turnover and accounts receivable turnover improves cash flow and we understand the concept of leverage. But in our worship of the bottom line we are too focused on cutting expenses. We will most likely hamper the sales effort since most accountants don't have the sales spirit. And finally, we're not real comfortable with the operations side of the business.

CONCLUSION

While the use of ratios and formulas in this chapter may not fit some people's reading styles, the basic message of this chapter is simple. The management decisions you make will influence the value of your business. One counterintuitive example is the use of debt. Many owners avoid debt believing that debt increases risk. But there are other risks that debt can reduce. Under some circumstances the use of debt can strengthen your company through a greater return on equity. If you never expand with debt, you may lose future market share to competitors, thus increasing your long-term risk. Especially if your personal strengths are on the sales or engineering sides, your accountant can help you use financial variables to strengthen your business now and in the future.

QUESTIONS TO ASK YOURSELF

1. Which of the above management styles best describes me?

2. What areas of my business require attention now?

3. Do I know what my top three customer critical success factors are?

4. How efficiently are the assets of my business being utilized?

5. Do I employ debt when it's logical to do so?

QUESTIONS TO ASK YOUR ACCOUNTANT

1. What is my return on equity and is it increasing or decreasing?

2. What are the key asset turnover ratios I need to watch?

3. Am I over-leveraged or under-leveraged?

4. How do my financial ratios stack up against my competitors?

5. Is my business more valuable now than it was two years ago?

CHAPTER 22

Enhancing the Value of Your Business (or preparing it for sale)

We are going to share some ideas about how to increase the value of your business. Our starting point is the base assumption that your business is not a publicly traded or professionally managed firm, but a closely-held or family-owned business. In the US, such businesses make up about 85% of all businesses and hold 65% of the value.

The easiest way to improve the value of your business is to treat it as if it were going to be for sale. The best way we know to approach systematically adding value is to start with the premise that you are getting the company ready to "show" to list with an investment banker who will tell the best story possible and get the best price and terms possible for you.

GETTING YOUR BUSINESS READY FOR "SALE"

You say that selling isn't in your plans; that you intend to give your business to your son or daughter or other family members?

Let's just pretend that you've decided it's time to sell what you created. (Or there may come a time when you *must* sell or your family must sell if you pass away.) One of the first things that a potential buyer will request is your company's financial statements and tax returns for the past several years. So naturally, you will want to make the business look as good as possible. Yet, minimizing the amount due in taxes, which makes good sense when you are running your business on a day-to-day basis, conflicts with showing higher profits. This creates a conundrum.

DO THE FIX-UP NOW

No one will pay to fix a business's past, current, or ongoing problems, nor will they pay you for opportunities that have not already been developed and exploited.

Selling your business can be a lot like selling your house. If the house hasn't been painted, cleaned, landscaped, and so on, it will sell for less than it would in top shape; as-is, it's a "fixer upper." The same concept applies to a business, except that it typically takes one to three years to get a business ready for sale. Whether you sell it or not, this gives you a reasonable timeline to work on your business. When you improve your business, you benefit from the improvements when you keep it or if you sell it.

A Few Words About *Hysterical* Financial Statements — What To Do?

No, it isn't a typographical error, it does say *hysterical*, not historical. We're talking about "cleaning-up" financial statements. Adjusting financial statements is a common and natural step in a business buyer's due diligence process. But what you adjust and why can be critical when making value considerations in the acquisition of a business.

Potential buyers will request your company's financial statements and tax returns for the past several years when you place the business up for sale. Convincing a potential buyer that your business has substantially more value will be an uphill battle when you have documented on tax returns, and probably in internally prepared financial statements, that the business has minimal income. Typically, in closely-held companies, compensation and perks to owners and managers tend to be based on the owners' personal desires and the company's ability to pay, rather than on the value of the services these individuals perform. So, if your business is very profitable but you drain off profits in high family salaries and benefits, your accountant can prepare restated financials for a buyer.

You have probably also seen or heard of a number of techniques to make income "disappear" for tax purposes. Please note that the tax collection agencies can question:

- The employment and provision of perks to family members who are not contributing an equivalent amount in time and effort to the business.

- Expensing automobiles that are primarily used for personal use
- Owners compensation that is significantly greater than what one would have to pay a "manager"
- Multiple owner perks:
  - Automobile insurance
  - Life, family health, dental, and disability insurance not provided to employees
  - Non-business related expenses including travel and entertainment, cleaning services, home improvements, and any number of expenditures that an owner may want to evade paying taxes on (note the word "evade," a motivation that is not looked upon favorably by tax collection agencies and owners may be loath to disclose)
- Transactions that involve company insiders:
  - Renting real estate at more (or less) than fair market value
  - Company loans to and from shareholders where there is no intent to repay any time soon
- Valuation of inventory at whatever it takes to make net income disappear
- Any non-recurring events that affect bottom-line results

Your financial statements may carry a number of accounts that haven't been looked at or reconciled for a number of years. This is most likely true if you do not engage an accountant on a regular basis to do at least a review of your financial statements and update the accounts accordingly. For example, inventory may be substantially overvalued because of "obsolete" inventory that needs to be removed. The accounts receivable and payable may not agree to the supporting ledgers, fixed assets may be over- or understated, and non-business and off-balance sheet related assets and liabilities may or may not be recorded. You will be amazed at what an accountant or knowledgeable business consultant can spot by simply analyzing your financial statements.

CONVINCING THAT "BUYER"

It is hard to build credibility with a buyer and convince them they should pay you a premium for your business when your financial statements show you "don't make much money." This demonstrates to the prospective buyer that there is substantial additional risk in acquiring your business because they will have to determine what is accurate and what isn't, and thus they will pay significantly less in order to compensate themselves for taking that risk. A key point to remember is that buyers do *not* like risk, and expect to be compensated for the risk they take by paying less for your business than you may think it is worth.

At some point in your life you will *have to* transfer your ownership to another person. Planning for it now will do more than make it easier when the time comes. By cleaning up your business processes and accounting now, you get the benefits of a better, more profitable business now *and* more value when it transfers. To use the real estate analogy again, by remodeling and upgrading your kitchen now, you get to enjoy it while you live in the house, and your house will sell for more later.

THE COUNTDOWN TO A BETTER BUSINESS (OR CASHING IN!)

Three years out:

1. Bite the bullet and engage an expert to perform an operational assessment. Such analyses can be performed by experienced business valuation professionals, accountants, or management consultants.

2. Accept that in order to earn top dollar in or for your business, you will have to focus on your business more

than you ever had to before. Make those improvements and investments you've been meaning to do.

3. Stop running non-business expenses through company accounts.

4. Don't be penny-wise and pound-foolish. Pay the additional tax on the increased net income, you will make it up many times in the increased sales price.

5. Now is the time to initiate any growth plans you have.

6. Start making a list of potential buyers.

One year out:

7. Have an update to your operational assessment performed.

8. Implement operational assessment recommendations that streamline the business.

9. Keep making a list of potential buyers.

Three to six months out:

10. If you don't already have one, engage an accountant to analyze your financial statements.

11. Verify that each balance sheet account agrees with the supporting ledgers.

12. Implement the accounting recommendations your accountant makes.

13. Sweep the front porch!

Now you have a cleaned up business that you can enjoy and that will be easier to pass on to family, or sell for the greatest profit.

In closing, we would like to share one of those little pieces that just sticks with you. A prominent family-business owner, Jim Ethier, Chairman of Bush Brothers Beans, recently related some of his thoughts about how their family made it to its fourth generation of family owners. He was inspired by a book by Professor Leon Danco in which the following twelve commandments were prominent. We felt they were worth sharing.

12 COMMANDMENTS FOR THE BUSINESS OWNER

1. Thou Shalt Share The Dream With Thy Family.

2. Thou Shalt Inform Thy Managers and Employees, "This Company Will Last Forever."

3. Thou Shalt Develop a Workable Organizational Structure and Make it Visible on a Chart.

4. Thou Shalt Continue To Improve Thy Management Knowledge, That of Thy Managers, and That of Thy Family.

5. Thou Shalt Institute an Orthodox Accounting System And Make Available the Data Therefrom to Thy Managers, Advisors, and Directors.

6. Thou Shalt Develop a Council of Competent Advisors.

7. Thou Shalt Submit Thyself to the Review of a Board of Competent Outside Directors.

8. Thou Shalt Choose Thy Successor(s).

9. Thou Shalt Be Responsible That Thy Successor(s) be Well Taught.

10. Thou Shalt Retire and Install Thy Successor(s) With Thy Powers Within Thy Lifetime.

11. Thou Canst Not Take It With Thee — So Settle Thy Estate Plans — Now.

12. Thou Shalt Apportion Thy Time To See That These Commandments Be Kept.

CONCLUSION

Working *on* your business means treating it like it was for sale. You'll have a business to be proud of — or get top dollar in a sale.

QUESTIONS TO ASK YOURSELF

1. Could I sell my business in the future for what it is actually worth?

2. Do I want to clean up my business?

3. Could my business go public in the future?

4. Would more accurate financials help me manage better?

5. Do I have dead inventory or accounts that need to be written off?

QUESTIONS TO ASK YOUR ACCOUNTANT

1. How would you recommend I clean up my business?

2. Should I quit taking "off-the-book" perks?

3. What's the easiest way to improve things over the next three years?

CHAPTER 23

Why Succession Planning
Is Important

Business owners often avoid thinking about succession planning for at least two obvious reasons: they may not want to give up control, or are afraid to, and it means thinking about their own mortality. Succession planning transfers ownership of a business under controlled circumstances. A comprehensive succession plan is the key to unlocking the door to your future financial success. Without proper planning and execution, you and your family's financial objectives and quality of life are put on hold.

The process of succession planning will often require financial planning professionals, estate and gift tax lawyers, accountants, and perhaps even merger and acquisition specialists and business valuation appraisers. Before you meet with these professional advisors, you need to understand the dynamics of your family-owned-and-managed business. A word of caution: Often a business is not as valuable as an owner believes it to be. Outsiders will value your business "by the numbers." They will seldom pay for intangibles. It cannot be overstated how important it is to have realistic expectations.

The goals of each owner of a family business are unique, so an effective succession strategy must meet your personal goals. An effective succession plan ensures financial security in your retirement while minimizing income and estate taxes, preserves the value of your business after transferring ownership to family members or an outside party, and keeps wealth distribution equitable for your children or heirs.

THREE "BUYERS" OF YOUR BUSINESS

Generally, when transferring a family owned business, the disposition falls into three possible categories:

- Transferring the business to your successor heirs
- Selling the business to your employees
- Selling the business to an unrelated third party

When transitioning your business to your heirs, consider first and foremost whether or not you have a spouse, children, or in-law capable of running your business. Going forward, family dynamics play an important role. Business owners are not always the best people to impartially judge their heir's capabilities. If a promising successor exists within the family gene pool, an effective gifting program needs to be started, which can be coupled with sales of company stock, issuance of different classes of stock, and creation of trusts. The advice of a knowledgeable estate and gift tax professional is paramount. Ownership benefits and management control can be separated. Owners often have multiple children, either involved or not in the business, and concerns about fair treatment will most likely arise. Also, your ability to step aside and allow your successor to make important decisions is critical to the success of the transition.

There are times when transfers to your spouse or children are not the answer. For example, if inadequate retirement financial resources do not allow you to live in a manner to which you have grown accustomed and there is no apparent successor within the family, then the sale of the business to a non-family member becomes the more appropriate transition route. You may sell to a select group of key employees, the entire employee group, or outside third parties. Your understanding of your future financial needs and wishes, coupled with a business valuation will enable you to entertain meaningful offers.

When selling to key employees in the organization, the employees may not have the financial resources to purchase the business. In these circumstances, there are options available in structuring the terms and conditions of the sale to enable both parties to achieve their goals. Installment sales and consulting agreements are excellent ways to provide a steady stream of cash flow to the seller, while transitioning the ownership to key employee(s).

Employee stock ownership plans (ESOPs) are a way for business owners to transition their business to the employees. A properly structured ESOP is designed to provide significant tax advantages to an owner in order to enable workers to attain ownership. Although not new, ESOPs are growing in popularity and provide the owner with a tax-advantaged method for allowing the continuity of the business.

Proper due diligence is a must when selling the business to an outside third party. When selling to either an unrelated and unknown buyer, or to a respected known competitor, you must ascertain their ability to purchase and successfully run your business. The wrong purchaser can drain the business and then default on the sales agreement, leaving you with a crippled business worth less than when you sold it. All aspects of the quality of the purchaser must be understood prior to sale to ensure that your future financial needs and wishes are met.

When transition is necessary, it is important for the owner to consider all of the options. In developing your transition strategy, family needs, retirement needs, and estate implications are of utmost importance. A succession plan with a well-thought-out strategy is essential to unlocking the door to future financial success for you, your family, and your company.

SUCCESS VS. FAILURE

A large family-owned mechanical contractor went about the transitioning of the family business early and with a logical approach. Recognizing that only one child had the required qualities of education and experience in the business to oversee many day-to-day operations, the owner began to execute an effective transition plan. The name of the mechanical contractor was already recognized in the metropolitan area. The owner formed a new company, changing the original name slightly. You Bet You Can, Inc. became the feeder company for You Bet You Can Service, Inc., which was owned entirely by the owner's child and heir apparent. Eventually, all new contracts were awarded through and performed by the new company. Financially this worked well. The original mechanical contractor company was not required to guarantee bonds and estate tax savings were accomplished. The owner's child, who possessed the necessary business capabilities to run the company, began building value and the original company's value was frozen. This owner wanted to be fair and equitable with his other children. So, while this transition of the business was taking place, the owner was annually gifting interests in real estate partnerships to his other children and shares in the original company to his successor.

In a less happy instance, one of our successful automobile dealership clients was owned and operated by a fair and equitable father of four children. He had procrastinated for years about putting a succession plan together and suddenly found himself in failing health. This owner then began the execution of an aggressive estate tax plan without full consideration of his transition strategy. As a result, over time his four children ended up as equal owners of the automobile dealership even though only one of the children had the necessary business acumen to successfully manage the dealership. Not surprisingly, all four children felt that they should receive a paycheck resulting from their new positions as owners, even though two of the children did not work at the dealership and the third only sporadically showed up to work. Within several years after the father died, the burden of running a large dealership was too much for the one child managing day-to-day operations, and the dealership was sold for less than its true value.

CONCLUSION

It's always better to plan the ownership succession or financial sale of a business ahead of time. Why not look into it today? Proper planning will help you save on taxes, increase the value of your business, and improve the odds of a successful transition. Your accountant and other experts can help you implement your wishes and insure your financial needs.

QUESTIONS TO ASK YOURSELF

1. Is now the time for me to map out and implement a succession plan; what if something happened to me tomorrow — could my business survive?

2. Who are the key people in my company, and how can I transfer control to them over time?

3. Where do I get proper training for my successor or heirs, to help them become successful?

4. Will an interim president or mentor fill the gap until my heir is ready to take charge and do they have the same passion for the business that I have?

5. Do I identify myself with my business? Will my business be able to operate independently from me? Will I be able to let go? What will I do after I am no longer in charge?

6. Will the milestones and transition dates of my succession plan be enough to motivate my successor or heir?

7. How should I take care of my other family members who will not be taking over the family business?

8. How should I take care of key employees who will not inherit the business?

9. How financially dependant will I be on the continued success of the business, and do the buyout terms sufficiently meet my plans and objectives?

10. Am I ready to sell?

QUESTIONS TO ASK YOUR ACCOUNTANT

1. Have you assisted other family-owned businesses in implementing successful succession plans?

2. What does the process of transitioning my business entail?

3. If I sell my business to a third party, how do I transfer this wealth to my heirs in the most tax effective manner?

4. If I sell my business, will the financial proceeds meet my financial needs?

5. Should I sell the assets or stock of my business?

6. In allocating the sale price, what are the benefits in receiving the bulk of the proceeds in the form of a sales price versus getting paid under a covenant not to compete?

7. Should I be gifting shares of my company to a child or children, and if so, when should I start?

8. If I give or sell the bulk of my business to one of my children, how can I equalize my distribution to the rest of my children?

9. How can the issuance of nonvoting stock benefit me in my transition?

10. Does insurance make sense when you look at the composition of my assets and my tax obligation?

CHAPTER 24

Investing Now and for Your Future

Investing in the stock market is difficult for most people. When you add bonds, foreign markets, commodities, and many other options into the mix, investing can seem more difficult than running your business. However, for retirement and long-term profits, stocks and other investments let you own a piece of your national or the world economy. For example, over long periods of time the US stock market has grown on average at about 10% a year. But you must be prepared to hold stocks for years and not panic when short-term circumstances look bad.

In this chapter we'll provide a very brief overview of the investment world. We'll suggest a few general guidelines to use when approaching your investments. We'll also suggest that you get help to aid your analyses and your objectivity. Unfortunately, most people invest backwards — they get most enthusiastic about investing when the market is at its high point, and they stay away from the market when stocks are depressed. This means they buy high and sell low because they don't have a clear investment philosophy.

Since the late 1990s, the stock market has had some decisive ups and downs. For instance, the high-tech bubble created very high gains in technology stocks through 2000. But many individuals lost up to 80% on their portfolios' value when the bubble burst. Even professionals and mutual funds often overweighted their portfolios in tech stocks and paid a price. Since that crash, the market has had periods of up, down, and level. If you react emotionally or try to compete with experts who spend full time analyzing the market, you may have difficulties. You'll be better off using your accountant or investment professionals to help you by providing both objectivity and expertise.

MARKET PHOBIAS

In addition to the complexities of investing, many people also have a phobia about the market. While the recent tech crash could have something to do with this, it actually goes back to the 1929 stock market crash. Most of our parents or grandparents were directly or indirectly influenced by the Great Depression that was signaled by the Crash of 1929. The idea that the stock market can crash "overnight" and wipe out security and wealth is part of Western culture. The fact that the market has more controls and safety devices today doesn't change this deep-seated phobia.

CHANGES SINCE 1929

Investing in stocks is much safer now than it was in 1929. In 1929 there was no Securities and Exchange Commission and similar agencies around the world to closely monitor the market. There were no government-sponsored retirement programs to provide minimum incomes. There was no automatic government insurance on multiple bank accounts. There was no 50% margin requirement. In other words, the market was much more risky in 1929 than it is today. However, that doesn't make success in the stock market easy. Careful management of your investments is still critical to your investment success. If you buy overpriced stocks because they are the next big thing, you can still lose 80% of your money just as many high-tech stocks did in the 1990s.

A RATIONAL MARKET

In general, stocks and other investments make up what is called an efficient market. This means that most investments are priced "correctly" most of the time. However, there are definitely exceptions where investments are over- or under-priced for periods of time.

The general point is that many people approach investing like a lottery. They invest on tips and emotion. They buy when the economy is up and investment gurus are touting the stock market, and sell when there's a bit of bad economic news. But if you invest rationally for the longer term, good companies that earn money consistently will tend to go up and companies that are losers will tend to go down.

We like to think of investments as Warren Buffet does. He looks at investments as if he were buying the company. An analogy on a smaller scale would be when a client asks his or her accountant to evaluate an investment in their friend's restaurant or other small business. If it is a going business, your accountant can check the expenses, the profits, and so on. Given his or her experience with other similar businesses, your accountant should be able to warn you about possible pitfalls in the investment. Similarly, if it's a stock, your accountant may help you analyze it, and help you to understand the business. Is it profitable? If you invested, how soon would you get a reasonable return on your investment? What are the risks?

WHY INVEST AT ALL?

If investing is difficult and risky, why not just keep your money in the bank or CDs and avoid investing altogether? One big reason is inflation. Inflation is a pernicious, hidden tax that drains wealth. There are good reasons why President Ronald Reagan said, "Inflation is as violent as a mugger, as frightening as an armed robber, and as deadly as a hit man." When you add in normal taxes and inheritance taxes, you need to make money to stay even. It can sound corny to your kids, but you may remember when bread and gasoline were both 25 cents! That's inflation. In the 1960s many people thought they would be comfortable retiring on $300 a month! To stay even, you need to have income and assets that are growing with the economy. That's what investing in the market can provide.

YOUR NEEDS AND RISK PROFILE

When you invest, you must first know yourself and your investment goals. On the practical side, you should know your needs. Are you retired now and need to assure that you don't outlive your money? Or do you have 20 years to invest for retirement. Do you have a significant estate to pass on? Do you need to pay for children's or grandchildren's college educations?

On the more psychological side, you should determine how much risk you're willing to take. Following are a few sample questions you should ask yourself. If you have an investment advisor (which we recommend), they should ask you similar questions.

Practical Issues

1. How soon will you need the money back that you invest?

    ☐ in less than a year   ☐ 6–10 years

    ☐ 1–2 years   ☐ longer than 10 years

    ☐ 3–5 years

2. Do you need income now from your investments?

    ☐ no

    ☐ yes

3. What return have you been getting on your savings or investments? _____

4. Do you have any large, new expenses coming up (such as college costs for children)? If yes, how much will you need, and when?

    $ _____   When? _____

Psychological Issues

5. Which would you prefer:

    ☐ an investment that could either lose 25% or gain 150% over 10 years?

    ☐ an investment that could lose nothing or gain 40% over 10 years?

6. If the stock market fell by 20% this year, and your stocks with it. Would you:

    ☐ feel bad and consider selling some/all stocks.

    ☐ be concerned and continue to watch the market.

☐ not worry, because the market is likely to go up again in the next few years.

"Scoring" Yourself. You should answer questions like those above simply to give you and your advisors some insight into your situation and feelings. For instance, if you can't tolerate your stocks going down occasionally, then you may want to invest in more secure investments such as government notes or CDs, although the growth of your money will be limited.

WHAT YOU NEED

Questions like those above help to analyze how much money you need for your lifestyle now and later. Many factors go into your needs and wants. Do you want to buy a second home or travel when you retire? How do you expect your health to hold up as you get older? Are you naturally thrifty, a spendthrift, or in the middle? Do you want a new car every year? What do you project inflation to be?

For instance, take insurance. If you are investing for retirement and other goals, major medical costs can derail your plans. That means that any financial plan must make sure you are adequately insured for health issues. Some investment plans will use life insurance or annuities. Yet these are generally not considered investments in the classic sense. Your advisors should analyze all your needs and protect you financially against all the possible contingencies you may face.

They should also help you decide how much you need to save or invest now and determine how much you want to spend in the future. Then you can invest now to achieve your goals. After such analysis, many realize that they aren't setting aside enough and they'll have to step up their investments to achieve their goals. This is essential information and it is better knowing this now than later when it's too late to do anything about it! When you are retired, we often recommend that you should only take out about 4% of your total assets every year to live on if you want to preserve your assets and cope with inflation. And the less you take out in the early years, the better off you'll be. Like compound interest in reverse, taking out too much money early can have a *big* negative effect on your net worth!

YOUR PORTFOLIO

Research shows that being in the right asset class is far more important than picking individual stocks. This means that asset allocation decisions are more important than individual stock picking. As a simple example let's take the ratio between stocks and bonds in your portfolio. If you are retired and have no other income, you might want 80% of your assets in safe bonds that pay a fixed return you can count on. But if you are young with many years before retirement, you might want 100% of your assets in stocks.

The biggest decision you and your advisor can make is how to allocate your investments across different types of assets (like the stocks vs. bonds example above). Once you've decided on portfolio allocation, you have lots of specific options.

There are many investments you can use to meet your objectives, more than any time in history. In addition to large cap, small cap, mid cap, value, speculative stocks, and so on, there are many foreign markets that are currently outperforming the US markets. There are tech stocks, preferred and convertible stocks, options, covered calls, commodities, real estate investment trusts (REITs), and more. And that's not even considering the many types of mutual funds and unit trusts.

Another aspect of your investment portfolio to consider is tax considerations. For instance, by putting high-profit investments in tax-advantaged retirement plans or using them as gifts, your after-tax results can be improved. While your accountant can be particularly helpful here, it is important that tax considerations not drive investment decisions, and vice versa. As a simple example, remember that it's better to make a dollar and pay taxes on it than to lose a dollar because it's tax deductible! Of course, in taking a profit on investments, making gains long term instead of short term is preferred, as long as it doesn't keep you in a stock that needs to be sold immediately.

MAKING THE MOST OF YOUR INVESTMENTS

This chapter can't give you personal investment advice for at least two reasons. First, we don't know your needs and situation. Second, advice can go out of date in a day, a month, or a year. There are many portfolio choices available from aggressive to conservative. The important thing to remember is that your portfolio is chosen for a purpose and that purpose relates to external events. In other words, don't buy, hold, and forget about it. The economy changes. Your circumstances in life change. Adjust your portfolio, and its risk, accordingly.

YOU AND YOUR ACCOUNTANT

Perhaps *the* classic investment approach is a Graham-and-Dodd value analysis. Similar to Warren Buffet today, Graham and Dodd focused on analyzing the true book value of companies and only buying stocks when their value was higher than their price.

Most accounting firms are not also investment advisors. However, your accountant is still in a good position to help you with your analysis and decisions. Accounting training can help you with "due diligence," with understanding the numbers that reflect an investment's value, with balancing risk against your personal investment objectives, and with tax considerations.

To the extent that your accountant also advises you on investments, you achieve "one-stop shopping" where taxes, financial planning, estate planning, and investments can be handled as an integrated whole by one trusted advisor.

Conclusion

There is nothing to be afraid of in investment markets if you approach them with a sound philosophy. You'll be involved with investment decisions for retirement, company pension plans, and current returns. Your accountant can help give you objective analyses about the value of investments when fads and other market forces tend to make people overly optimistic or pessimistic.

Questions To Ask Yourself

1. Have I paid attention to my investments?

2. Have I been careful about investing when stocks are high?

3. Have I balanced my portfolio in the direction I need for growth vs. risk avoidance?

4. Have I thought about the long term?

5. Have I analyzed how much income I'll need for retirement?

6. Have I found advisors I trust to help me?

Questions To Ask Your Accountant

1. Are you comfortable helping me analyze investments?

2. If not, can you recommend an advisor you trust?

3. Can you calculate how much money I need to put aside now to have what I want when I retire?

CHAPTER 25

Planning for Your Legacy and Avoiding Estate Problems

You have worked hard to create and maintain your wealth. You very likely have a strong desire to have your business and family wealth continue. With proper estate planning, they can.

There are lots of excuses to put off estate planning, but simple inertia may be the biggest. Most individuals worry they won't have enough money to continue their current lifestyle if they do estate planning now. But estate planning doesn't mean you have to retire now on what you have. The earlier you begin planning, the better off you'll be later. Many people fear losing control of their assets or that their goals and desires will not be met or understood. In fact, good estate planning will help you reach your goals whether they are wealth retention or transfer, or both.

Do You Have Estate Tax Issues?

Many people's first reaction is "I don't have an estate tax issue." Maybe you don't, but there are other valuable reasons to make sure your legacy is continued. Here are 13 common problems that can destroy your wealth.

1. Predators, Creditors, and Lawsuits May Consume Your Assets. In today's society, minor accidents, business mistakes, the changing economy, environmental contamination, or a slip of the tongue may expose your entire wealth and nest egg to voluntary and involuntary creditors. Even if the claims are unfair, you can still end up paying huge expenses and suffering from the wasted time involved in confrontations. The test is: If you ran into a busload of brain surgeons and were sued, would your estate survive the litigation tornado that ensued?

2. Estate Taxes Could Eat Half of Your Estate. After working all of your life and paying income taxes, the government may come in and gobble up over 50% of your wealth in estate taxes. In some states, you may even have to pay inheritance taxes in addition to estate taxes and lose as much as 65%!!! The test is: If you and your spouse both died today in an airplane crash, what would happen to your estate? Remember, you must pay estate taxes with cash!

3. Probate Fees and Delays Will Eat Your Cash. Suffering through probate means having to go to court for a death probate when you or a family member dies, or for a disability probate when you or a family member becomes disabled. The average cost to a family going through probate is 5–7% of the total wealth of the deceased. You will incur attorney's fees, personal representative's fees, appraisal fees, accounting fees, and court costs. Plus your estate is in the public records for anyone to see. You may also be exposed to multiple probates on each family member on death or disability in multiple states and countries where you own real property.

4. Family Squabbles Can Split the Family. So many times, unnecessary lawsuits crop up among family members for emotional reasons. When discomforts cannot be contained, family members find themselves in court. Family breakups and feuds may cost your estate and continue through many generations.

5. Without Emergency Legal and Medical Documents You or Your Family May Suffer. Many of the delays, heartache, and pain resulting from medical disasters may be prevented with basic family-estate documents such as wills, living wills, durable medical powers of attorney, durable general powers of attorney, and funeral and burial instructions.

6. Unnecessary Paperwork Will Frustrate You. Does your family possess disorganized paperwork, incomprehensible files, multiple filings, too many bank accounts, and general paper disorganization? This can create a nightmare for you or your estate when you have to prove your case, or just execute your desires.

7. Insufficient Insurance Will Leave You Exposed. It is as much the job of your accountant and attorney as it is of insurance professionals to ensure that all protective insurance is in place before disaster (for example, death, disability, destruction, or a lawsuit) strikes the family. Life insurance is the mortar between the bricks of your estate!

8. Your Children Will Be Angry If You Leave a Mess for Them. Some businesses and estates are so messed up and disorganized that, when the father and mother die, the children refuse to become personal representatives and are angry at their deceased parents at a time when they need help to be calm.

9. What Good Is Money If It Spoils Your Children? The money you have today may spoil your children unless you place it in a Revocable Family Trust with your Statement of Wishes incorporated into the trust. You will not help your children by throwing money at them at arbitrary times (when they reach age 18, 25, 30, 35, etc.). A fixed-distribution schedule leaves open the possibility that money might reach your kids when they are in jail, in bankruptcy proceeding, in the middle of a divorce, lawsuit, or on drugs.

10. You Do Not Want to Lose Control of Your Assets. Most clients want to maintain control of their assets for as long as they live. It is okay for them to transfer "ownership" but not "control." Loss of control results in disappointment, depression, loneliness, and unsupervised disasters.

11. Cash Claustrophobia Can Terrorize Your Old Age. As people become older, their security blanket is the ready access to cash. When they sense that access to cash is too complicated or requires explanations, approvals, or multiple steps, they suffer from "cash claustrophobia." Sometimes they load up on inefficient, non-interest-bearing checking accounts as security blankets.

12. Inflation *Will* Dilute What You Have. You've often heard that nothing is certain except death and taxes. In recent decades, we can add inflation to that. Inflation creeps up on us at average rates of between 3–5% a year, reducing the value of your wealth, increasing your cost of living and reducing your buying power. Inflation is a given and it's deceptively invisible to most people. It also automatically increases your estate taxes.

13. Bad Marriages Can Destroy Bad Planning. What good is wealth if you lose half of it in a divorce? (See Chapter 26.) Does it feel good to give gifts and inheritance to a child only to have it filter to a non-deserving son-in-law or daughter-in-law? Your heart and soul will bleed when you imagine that your cute and deserving grandchildren will be raised by a son-in-law or daughter-in-law with bad habits, bad values, or bad character.

GOOD NEWS — ALL OF THESE PROBLEMS ARE PREVENTABLE WITH THE CORRECT MOVES

Every one of the above problems is preventable using proper structures and planning. There is no excuse for not being 100% protected. All of these issues can be resolved through proper estate planning and legacy planning. If any of the above issues applied to you, seek assistance now.

Estate planning is not a one-size-fits-all process. We believe your estate plan has to be tailor made to meet your goals and desires. This customization takes more effort, but equates to a better end result for you. Make sure your accountant and attorney have a process, not a cookie cutter approach, to ensure your needs are met. It could take several meetings with your advisors as well as good communication to ensure success. Our suggestions follow.

The Discovery Process. Understanding your personal and family goals and desires is the first key to achieving your goals. Look for solutions to any obstacles that are discovered. This ensures selection of the best estate planning tools to achieve your goals.

Gaining confidence that your current life style will not be altered is your next step. You worked hard to get to this point in your life, and it is time to enjoy it. Your accountant or other professional should give you cash projections, using your information, to make sure you have enough money to live on.

Next you assess your current tax situation by determining your actual current estate tax that would be due now and the estate tax due at your predicted actuarial date of death. Most people are shocked at the amount of tax that will be due.

The Plan and the Path. Once you have a clear understanding of your goals and desires you can move ahead with the planning process. Your accountant can design your legacy, integrating various estate-planning tools to reach your goals.

Schedule a family meeting to communicate the plan to those involved.

Implementation. The implementation begins when the plan is finalized and approved. Talk to your advisor about drafting the documents. Your accountant can also advise you on gifting, if desired, and make sure it is completed.

Completion. Celebrate your accomplishment!! This is not an easy process to go through, but once completed, you will feel a sense of peace knowing your legacy will be passed on to future generations.

It's a good idea to meet with your accountant annually to update your plan for your ever-changing goals and to cover any tax law changes.

DOING IT RIGHT

Beth came to us devastated; she had just lost her parents and was still adjusting to the loss. To make matters worse, her parents had not done an adequate job of estate planning; now Beth was faced with having to come up with $250,000 in estate taxes. She did receive many assets, but most were tied up and she didn't have any available cash to pay the taxes. She was angry, not understanding how her parents could leave her in this position; after all, her father was a bright, successful businessman. We were able to help Beth sell some of her personal assets to pay the estate taxes. This process took several years however. Beth never forgot the pain of that process, and vowed not to make her kids go through the same experience.

Beth, now 80, is content knowing her kids will not have to endure the same frustrations. Here are the benefits Beth knows are in place:

- $10 million dollars in assets has been moved out of her estate.
- She still has control over certain assets that are dear to her.
- Funded several charities — these charities will receive money to continue her legacy and vision for years to come. Her kids are active as her foundation board, so they too will know their mother's wishes.
- Set up trusts for the kids so creditors and predators will not be able to get the money intended for the family.

This process took several years to get into place, and is still reviewed and adjusted annually to meet her wishes and make certain the plan is in line with the current laws. She reminds her kids often that they will not have to endure the frustration she went through, and encourages them to start their own legacy planning early for their families.

It is your choice — what legacy do you want to leave?

CONCLUSION

Every business must be sold or passed on to others at some point. If you deal with the process now instead of putting it off, you will be able to ensure that your wishes are carried out. You will also avoid leaving a mess to others at a time when they are least able to deal with it. Proper planning can save you lots of money in capital gains or estate taxes. Handled right, the whole succession process can be satisfying and profitable instead of messy and unpleasant.

QUESTIONS TO ASK YOURSELF

1. How much money do I have to live on the rest of my life?

2. As a couple, have we discussed our:

   - Personal goals
   - Family goals
   - Charitable goals

3. Do I have a strong estate plan?

4. Am I facing the family issues and obstacles, or leaving them for someone else to deal with?

QUESTIONS TO ASK YOUR ACCOUNTANT

1. Do I have enough money to live on for the rest of my life?

2. Do you do estate planning or work with someone who does?

3. If I were to die tomorrow, would I have an estate tax problem?

4. Do you know a good estate-planning attorney?

5. What is your process of estate planning to ensure that my wishes and my family's needs are addressed?

CHAPTER 26

Divorce and the
Small-Business Owner

Strong marriages and successful businesses both require good communication and plenty of attention to survive. When either your business or your marriage ends prematurely it is very stressful on the other. The purpose of this chapter is to highlight some of the issues that impact small business owners when there is a divorce and help you avoid or deal with them.

GOOD COMMUNICATION IS NEEDED

In most cases, only one spouse is actively involved in the business. As a result, the other spouse may become anxious about the financial impact the divorce will have on them and their continuing financial security. Where there are concerns that one spouse may try to hide assets from the other spouse, business "secrets" can be protected with a confidentiality agreement. If divorce is imminent, then your accountant should be directed to coordinate full disclosure of business operations. Your accountant can serve as the liaison between the company's in-house accounting staff and the experts for the parties to the divorce. The business's current financial condition, plans for the future, and its historical economic benefit directly or indirectly to the owner or owners who are a party to the divorce, will be instrumental in determining the level of financial support available and the value of the business in settling the property division.

Your accountant and attorney may also be called on to aid in tracing ownership, should the business pre-date the marriage or if ownership was succeeded by gift or inheritance. They may also aid the experts for each spouse in determining the true income of the owners, as well as understanding shareholder agreements, retirement plans, health benefits, buy-sell agreements, or a myriad of other contractual agreements or obligations of the company and its shareholders.

The importance of open communication and cooperation in discovery about your business cannot be overemphasized. The business's accountant, attorney, retirement plan administrator, insurance agent, and other professionals need to educate the experts and facilitate the efficient and thorough flow of information. The level of cooperation needed must be mandated from day one by the spouse in a position to do so. Even this level of cooperation may not completely put aside the anxiety or suspicions of the other spouse, but it will keep a costly process from becoming ridiculously expensive. If the experts are afforded full discovery, accurate financial data will be forthcoming. Additionally, the experts for the spouse not in the business can provide reassurance that he or she is getting a fair shake.

VALUATION AND TAX ISSUES

Within an atmosphere of cooperation, the business's ownership interests can be fairly valued. The level of the employee/owner spouse's income and related economic benefits can be determined. All of these decisions can produce different tax results now and in the future. Both spouses and all professionals should work for a structure that is most tax efficient to the marital estate. Remember that the economic unit called "family" prior to the divorce survives the legal unwinding of the marriage.

The myriad tax-related issues are too complex to analyze in this article. It is, however, important to remember to consider both the current and future tax consequences of the settlement. Ownership can be transferred incident to a divorce without current taxation. Your tax basis is not changed. The spouse retaining ownership must understand the tax consequences of a future disposition of the assets in a taxable transaction.

Often the value of a party's interest in a small business is in excess of other marital assets available to satisfy the property settlement. Use of an installment note involves tax issues related to interest paid on receivables and collateral. The tax consequences related to retirement assets should also be considered and communicated by the experts to their respective clients. A well-managed small business will have in place a financial management reporting system and succession planning documents. The succession planning documents should address the effect of divorce on ownership.

Business valuation in a divorce environment will in most cases differ from other valuation assignments. The professional hired to value the business must be an expert in the field of business valuations. Beyond that, however, the valuation analyst must understand the impact on value of many divorce-specific state or provincial statutes and court cases. Marital versus non-marital ownership issues may be present. Personal versus business goodwill may be an issue and this is not just an issue in professional service businesses. Income for support can become an area of concern to avoid double counting as an adjustment to the income stream in valuing the business. Inherent in every valuation assignment will be the valuation date and the standard of value.

The valuation date is often the date of filing for divorce, but this may be state or province specific. As to the standard of value, "value" is interpreted in a myriad of ways and can be state or province specific or even vary by the judge presiding over the case. Most statutes use the term "value" without precise definition. Consequently, each state or province's case law will have to be considered and understood.

OTHER ISSUES

After standard of value, one of the most contentious issues in matrimonial valuation assignments may well be "reasonable compensation":

- What it is
- Its impact on value versus support
- How to avoid double counting

The double-dip can occur if the divorcing owner's salary or other economic benefits are normalized downward to reflect market conditions, thus increasing the value of the business. Then if actual earnings and benefits are used to determine support, a double-dip can occur. How this can be addressed will vary based on the jurisdiction.

Among the many other issues to consider will be:

- *Professional Licenses.* In some jurisdictions, the value of a professional license is considered an asset separate and apart from the professional practice.

- *Degrees.* Educational degrees can be property subject to division. The valuation process is similar to a business interruption claim. Compare expected lifetime income with and without the degree; determine an appropriate discount rate to bring the stream of income to present value. Where allowed by the courts, this is often an issue when one spouse has worked to put the other through school.

- *Celebrity Goodwill.* Similar to a degree, the measure of value is the enhanced earning power of a celebrity and may be divisible as property as well as a source of support payments.

- *Covenants Not to Compete.* Many jurisdictions treat a covenant as personal goodwill and, thus, not a marital asset for property division. However, the income may be counted for support.

- *Buy-Sell Agreements.* A buy-sell agreement may or may not be respected in a divorce settlement. Even if the agreement was bargained for in an arm's length manner, state or provincial statutes and case law will need to be understood.

- *Stock Exemptions.* Once value is decided, transfer of ownership between spouses often is required to carry out the agreement. A stock redemption is complicated and requires special care, but it could be a method to use business liquidity to accomplish the settlement. This liquidity can often be achieved at favorable capital gains rates if done properly.

- *Retirement Plans.* Retirement plans are often a major asset in a divorce. These plans must also be valued. The valuation procedure and the complexity of the assignment will vary by the type of plan. The division of retirement assets will often mandate the use of a "Qualified Domestic Relations Order" (QDRO). A QDRO is a court order directing the administrator of a qualified plan to award a portion of the participant's interests in the plan to a spouse or dependent, pursuant to a divorce. In a small business, retirement plans come in many forms. Each type of plan will require varying valuation methods and analysis, but there is one common thread: Do it wrong and the tax costs will increase. The parties must understand the current and future tax costs in light of the overall property settlement.

BOB AND CAROL AND TED AND ALICE

Bob and Carol had grown apart over the years, but they still respected each other. Carol had been a big supporter when the business got started and then spent most of her energy raising the kids. After the kids were gone, they had little to hold them together. Without going into specifics, events occurred which made divorce the outcome. They had an adequate prenuptial agreement and, despite tendencies to assign blame, both Bob and Carol wanted a "friendly" divorce and their grown children encouraged that. Carol trusted Bob's accounting because she knew he had well-prepared financials and had never twisted them to advantage. Bob was willing to split their net worth equally and Carol was willing to accept terms and become a creditor of the business. Both parties were satisfied with the settlement and they were able to remain friendly after the divorce at family get-togethers.

At the other extreme, Ted and Alice fought over the divorce like they had fought during the marriage. Alice knew that Ted had played games with his accounting over the years to cheat on their income taxes and she didn't trust any figures he gave her. They had no prenuptial agreement and their personal styles were opposite. One expected hard bargaining, low-ball offers, and conflict. The other wanted to get it done but didn't want to be cheated. At one point Ted considered walking away from the business, running off with the assets that he could grab, and leaving Alice with what was left. After two years of expensive litigation, the settlement left both parties unhappy and the business had to be sold to cover the debt.

CONCLUSION

Valuation of business interests is a complex process to start with. Adding emotional issues and matrimonial litigation into the mix further adds to the need for expert assistance. There are many complex and interrelated business, tax, and valuation issues to deal with in a divorce. Add a small business to the marital estate and the level of complexity is greatly increased and the need for expert help is further enhanced. Please note that Federal and State or Province laws must be addressed. This article is not a comprehensive outline or checklist for small business owners, but is intended instead to motivate you to implement a delayed "prenuptial" agreement if possible and plan ahead to save taxes and conflict. Implementing a delayed agreement can often be done without raising suspicions by making it part of a comprehensive estate plan. Contact your own professional advisors when faced with a divorce.

QUESTIONS TO ASK YOURSELF

1. Do you have an agreement with your spouse in case of divorce?

2. Should I have a discussion with my spouse about details of the business?

3. Can I document anything now that would help me in case of divorce?

QUESTIONS TO ASK YOUR ACCOUNTANT

1. Can I create a business valuation formula ahead of time that is accepted in case of divorce?

2. Have you worked with divorce valuations for my kind of business?

3. Can you recommend other advisors in case of divorce?

Afterword

In compiling this book, it was our distinct intent to raise questions about areas of your business that you may not have explored yet and to create an awareness of opportunities where our expertise may be of service to you as we build a stronger relationship. We want to be your most trusted business advisors and help you shape your business so that you may experience great joy and achieve greater success in all that you do for your business and your family.

Contributing Authors

Everyone Knows What Accounting Services Are – Don't They?
Whalen & Company, CPAs
Richard D. Crabtree, CPA
Worthington, Ohio

Who Needs Accounting Systems?
Taketa, Iwata, Hara & Associates, LLC
Janet Hara, CPA
Hilo, Hawaii

Your Family Business History: Past and Future
SBLR LLP Chartered Accountants
Howard Lerner, CA, FCA (UK)
Toronto, Ontario

What Form of Business Should I Use?
Gollob, Morgan, Peddy & Co., P.C.
Tony K. Morgan, CPA & Robert W. Peddy, CPA
Tyler, Texas

Business Process Documentation: Key People and Processes
Croft, Drozd & Company, P.C.
Cecilia Loose, CPA
Exton, Pennsylvania

Strategic Planning and Competition
Coker James & Company, P.C.
Joseph S. James, CPA
Atlanta, Georgia

Why Budgeting and Planning Are Important
Whitley Penn
Dallas, Texas

Helping Your Managers Budget
Enterprise Network Worldwide
Nashville, Tennessee

Controller Services
Enterprise Network Worldwide
Kevin M. Poppen, CPA
Nashville, Tennessee

The Value of Audited Financials
Blankenship CPA Group, PLLC
Claude Blankenship, CPA
Nashville, Tennessee

Year-End Tax Planning
Cohen Friedman Dorman Leen & Co.
Jerry Bobal, CPA
Clark, New Jersey

Tax Return Preparation for the Family Business
Enterprise Network Worldwide
Kevin M. Poppen, CPA
Nashville, Tennessee

The R&D Tax Credit – It's Not Just for High-Tech Companies
alliantgroup LP
Justin Goodson, Steffanie Gunn, & Erin Meyer
Houston, Texas

Cost Segregation: "Extra" Depreciation for You
GranthamPoole CPAs /
Construction Economics, LLC
John McCallum, CPA
Jackson, Mississippi

Intellectual Property
The Rainmaker Academy
Charlie Flood, ME
Nashville, Tennessee

Working with Banks
Orizon Group, Inc.
Craig Wilkins
Omaha, Nebraska

Marketing Is More than You Think
Detweiler, Hershey & Associates, P.C.
Kenneth Byler, Director of Marketing
Souderton, Pennsylvania

Referrals Build Your Business
Enterprise Network Worldwide
Nashville, Tennessee

**It's a People Business:
Employee Benefits**
Enterprise Network Worldwide
Kristin L. Gentry, Associate Director
Nashville, Tennessee

**Why Your Business Retirement Plan
Is Important**
DeBoer, Baumann & Company, PLC
George M. Gardner, Jr., CPA
Holland, Michigan

Analyzing the Value of Your Business
Seidel, Schroeder & Company
Stephen M. Gonsoulin, CPA, ASA, CBA
Brenham, Texas

Enhancing the Value of Your Business
Coulter & Justus, PC
David G. Moser, ASA, CEI
Knoxville, Tennessee

Why Succession Planning Is Important
Councilor, Buchanan & Mitchell, P.C., CPAs
Peter B. Reilly, CPA, CVA
Bethesda, Maryland

Investing Now and For Your Future
Orizon Group, Inc.
Dan Tucker
Omaha, Nebraska

**Planning for Your Legacy and
Avoiding Estate Problems**
Pottroff Accountancy Corporation
Harley Pottroff, CPA
Manhattan, Kansas

Divorce and the Small-Business Owner
Pratt-Thomas & Gumb, CPAs
Melissa J. Johnson, CPA, CVA
Charleston, South Carolina

Index